303 'Round the Clock Recipes

Barbara's Open-House Waffles, page 35

Chicken Quesadillas El Grande, page 182

Apple-Pork Chop Casserole, page 271

Gooseberry Patch
2545 Farmers Dr., #380
Columbus, OH 43235

www.gooseberrypatch.com
1·800·854·6673

Copyright 2014, Gooseberry Patch 978-1-62093-144-8
First Printing, February, 2014

Check out our cooking videos on YouTube!

 Scan this code with your smartphone or tablet…it takes you right
to our YouTube playlist of cooking videos for **303 'Round the Clock
Recipes**. While there, you can also view our entire collection of
Gooseberry Patch cooking videos!

 If you spot this icon next to a recipe name, it means we created a video
for it. You'll find it at **www.youtube.com/gooseberrypatchcom**

Your exclusive ticket to

a Gooseberry Patch adventure!

When a new season is drawing near, there's nothing more exciting than pulling out favorite recipes and getting inspired. As an **exclusive, free gift** for Gooseberry Patch email subscribers, Vickie and JoAnn are creating **limited edition collections** of the very best of the seasons.

These handcrafted seasonal guides (**$9.95 value**) are full of our favorite recipes, inspiring photos, DIY tips and holiday ideas – you'll be celebrating all season long! A new issue will be released 4 times per year and each one is available for a limited time only.

If you haven't signed up yet, come aboard. Your subscription is your ticket to year 'round inspiration – and it's completely free!

www.gooseberrypatch.com/signup

Visit our website today, add your name to our email list, and you'll be able to download our latest seasonal preview instantly!

Find Gooseberry Patch wherever you are!
www.gooseberrypatch.com

Call us toll-free at 1·800·854·6673

Be a part of our bestselling cookbooks.

Share your tried & true recipes on our website and you'll be considered for our upcoming titles. If selected, your recipe will be printed along with your name and hometown. You'll even receive a FREE copy of the cookbook when it's published!

CONTENTS

101 BREAKFAST & BRUNCH RECIPES

101 SOUPS, SALADS & SANDWICHES

CONTENTS

101 COZY CASSEROLES

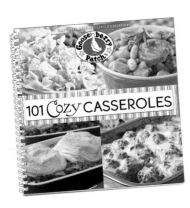

Family-Favorite Corn Soufflé, page 275

Cranberry Hootycreek Pancakes, page 37

Pioneer Beef Stew, page 126

Melon-Berry Bowls, page 23

Potato Doughnuts, page 90

Make-Ahead Breakfast Eggs, page 60

Orange-Cinnamon French Toast, page 51

101 Breakfast & Brunch Recipes

Grandma's Warm Breakfast Fruit, page 63

Pennsylvania Dutch Scrapple, page 75

Bacon & Egg Potato Skins, page 43

Get those sleepyheads out of bed with an amazing breakfast or brunch...they're sure to start each day off right!

Easy Breakfast Squares, page 82

Butterscotch Granola, page 19

French Toast Casserole, page 62

Tips for Easy-Breezy Breakfast Meals

★ A delicious way to perk up a bowl of oatmeal…stir in a tablespoon or two of canned pumpkin. Top with a sprinkle of pumpkin pie spice. Good and good-for-you!

★ Love cheesy scrambled eggs, overstuffed omelets and other egg dishes, but you're always too sleepy or short on time to fix them for breakfast? Good news…they're yummy at dinnertime too!

★ Pancake breakfasts are a favorite small-town tradition, often held at a local elementary school, church or grange hall. Watch for announcements in your newspaper for this fun annual event.

★ Surprise sleepyheads at breakfast…serve each a made-to-order omelet in a mini cast-iron skillet. A cheery red bandanna tied around the handle makes a nice, big napkin.

★ Mix pancake or waffle batter in a wide-mouth, spouted pitcher, then pour right onto the griddle…less dishes to wash!

★ Bacon is so tasty, but can be messy to fry…bake it instead! Lay bacon slices on a jelly-roll pan and bake at 350 degrees for 15 to 20 minutes, until it's as crisp as you like. Drain well on paper towels.

Break-of-Day Berry Parfait

1 c. strawberries, hulled and
   sliced
1/2 c. raspberries
1/4 c. blackberries
1 c. bran & raisin cereal
6-oz. container strawberry
   yogurt

In a bowl, combine berries; divide
into 2 small bowls. Top each with
cereal. Spoon yogurt over top.
Serves 2.

9

Michelle Case
Yardley, PA

So pretty served in a
parfait or champagne glass!

Kelly's Easy Caramel Rolls

3 T. corn syrup, divided
3 T. brown sugar, packed and
   divided
3 T. chopped pecans, divided
2 T. butter, cubed and divided
12-oz. tube refrigerated biscuits

To each of 10 greased muffin cups, add one teaspoon each of syrup, brown sugar and pecans. Top each with 1/2 teaspoon butter and one biscuit. Bake at 400 degrees for 8 to 10 minutes, until golden. Invert rolls onto a plate before serving. Makes 10 rolls.

Kelly Marshall
Olathe, KS

This is a much-requested
family recipe!

Frosty Orange Juice

6-oz. can frozen orange juice
    concentrate, partially thawed
1 c. milk
1 c. water
1 t. vanilla extract
1/3 c. sugar
12 ice cubes

Process all ingredients together in a blender until frothy. Serve in tall glasses. Makes 4 servings.

Tiffany Classen
Wichita, KS
Thick, frosty and
very refreshing!

II

Grab & Go Breakfast Cookies

1/2 c. butter, softened
1/2 c. sugar
1 egg, beaten
2 T. frozen orange juice
    concentrate, thawed
1 T. orange zest
1-1/4 c. all-purpose flour
1 t. baking powder
1/2 c. wheat & barley cereal

Blend together butter and sugar in a
bowl until light and fluffy. Beat in
egg, orange juice and zest; set aside.
Combine flour and baking powder in
a small bowl; stir into butter mixture
until blended. Stir in cereal. Drop
by tablespoonfuls, 2 inches apart,
on an ungreased baking sheet. Bake
at 350 degrees for 10 to 12 minutes,
until golden around edges. Cool on
a wire rack. Makes 1-1/2 dozen.

Penny Sherman
Cumming, GA

These cookies are perfect for
those busy mornings when you
have to rush out the door.

Milk & Honey Couscous

2 c. milk
2 T. honey
1 T. cinnamon
2 c. couscous, uncooked
1/3 c. dried apricots, chopped
1/3 c. raisins
1/2 c. slivered almonds

Combine milk, honey and cinnamon in a saucepan over medium heat. Bring to a boil; stir in couscous. Remove from heat; cover and let stand for 5 minutes. Fold in remaining ingredients. Serves 6.

13

Melanie Lowe
Dover, DE

This quick-to-fix breakfast is perfect for those chilly mornings when you need something to fill you up and keep you warm.

Slow-Cooker Breakfast Casserole

32-oz. pkg. frozen diced potatoes
1 lb. bacon, diced and cooked
1 onion, diced
1 green pepper, diced
1/2 c. shredded Monterey Jack
   cheese
1 doz. eggs
1 c. milk
1 t. salt
1 t. pepper

Layer 1/3 each of potatoes, bacon,
onion, green pepper and cheese.
Repeat layers 2 more times, ending
with a layer of cheese. In a bowl, beat
together eggs, milk, salt and pepper.
Pour over mixture in slow cooker.
Cover and cook on low setting for
8 to 9 hours. Serves 8 to 10.

Felice Jones
Boise, ID

This is a perfect recipe for
busy mornings. You wake up,
the house smells so good
and breakfast is ready as
soon as you are.

Honeyed Fruit & Rice

2 c. cooked jasmine rice
1/3 c. dried cranberries
1/3 c. dried apricots, chopped
1/4 c. honey
Garnish: milk

Stir together hot cooked rice,
cranberries, apricots and honey.
Divide into 2 bowls; top with milk.
Makes 2 servings.

15

Marilyn Epley
Stillwater, OK

Jasmine rice is also known
as fragrant rice and can
be found in many markets
or specialty stores.

Cheese & Chive Scrambled Eggs

6 eggs, beaten
1/4 t. lemon pepper
1 T. fresh chives, chopped
1/8 t. garlic salt
1 T. butter
1/3 c. shredded Colby Jack cheese
1/3 c. cream cheese, softened

In a bowl, combine eggs, pepper, chives and salt; set aside. Melt butter in a skillet over medium-low heat; add egg mixture. Stir to scramble, cooking until set. Remove from heat; stir in cheeses until melted. Serves 2 to 3.

Deborah Wells
Broken Arrow, OK

Paired with crisp bacon and hot biscuits, this is one dish we love so much I've even served it for dinner!

Johnny Appleseed Toast

4 slices cinnamon-raisin bread
1-1/2 T. butter, divided
1 Gala apple, cored and sliced
4 t. honey
1 t. cinnamon

Spread each slice of bread with one teaspoon of butter. Cover each bread slice with an apple slice; drizzle with one teaspoon honey and sprinkle with cinnamon. Place topped bread slices on an ungreased baking sheet. Broil on high for one to 2 minutes, until toasted and golden. Makes 4 servings.

17

**Rebekah Spooner
Huntsville, AL**

I'm a teacher, and we make this every fall to celebrate Johnny Appleseed with our little ones in September.

Feel-Good Shake

2 bananas, sliced
2 c. milk
2 c. non-fat vanilla yogurt
1 c. pineapple juice
1 T. honey

Process all ingredients together in a blender until smooth. Pour into a tall glass. Serve immediately. Makes 2 to 4 servings.

Patti Boepple
Trinidad, CO

This shake is a perfect way to start your day. One sip and you'll be hooked.

Butterscotch Granola

10 c. long-cooking oats,
  uncooked
2 sleeves graham crackers,
  crushed
2 c. sweetened flaked coconut
1 c. pecans, finely chopped
3/4 c. brown sugar, packed
1 t. baking soda
1 t. salt
2 c. butter, melted
16-oz. pkg. butterscotch chips

Mix together all ingredients except butterscotch chips in a deep, greased 13"x9" baking pan or a roaster pan. Bake at 300 degrees for 40 minutes, stirring every 10 minutes. Add butterscotch chips during the last 5 minutes; mix well after melted to distribute evenly. Cool. Store in an airtight container. Makes 5 quarts.

19

Alicia Sauvageau
East Wenatchee, WA

This is the best granola I have ever eaten. My kids and husband love it over berry yogurt!

Busy-Morning Banana Bread

3 ripe bananas, mashed
3 eggs, beaten
1/2 c. butter, melted and slightly
   cooled
1 T. vanilla extract
1/2 c. water
18-1/2 oz. pkg. yellow cake mix

In a large bowl, blend together
bananas, eggs, butter, vanilla and
water. Gradually add dry cake mix.
Beat with an electric mixer on high
speed for 4 minutes. Pour batter into
2 greased 9"x5" loaf pans. Bake at
350 degrees for 40 minutes. Increase
temperature to 400 degrees and bake
an additional 5 to 10 minutes, until
tops are golden. Makes 2 loaves.

Laura Justice
Indianapolis, IN
Super easy and freezes well.
Just pull from the freezer
the night before and
it will be ready for
your busy morning!

Huevos Rancheros to Go-Go

2 c. green tomatillo salsa
4 eggs
1-1/2 c. shredded Monterey Jack
   cheese
4 8-inch corn tortillas

Lightly coat a skillet with non-stick
vegetable spray and place over
medium heat. Pour salsa into skillet;
bring to a simmer. With a spoon,
make 4 wells in salsa and crack an
egg into each well, taking care not to
break the yolks. Reduce heat to low;
cover and poach eggs for 3 minutes.
Remove skillet from heat and top
eggs with cheese. Transfer each egg
with a scoop of salsa to a tortilla.
Serves 2 to 4.

Tonya Sheppard
Galveston, TX
These are a favorite around
my house...all the yummy
ingredients for a great
breakfast are wrapped up
in a handy tortilla.

Bowl-Free Cereal-to-Go

1/4 c. sugar
1/2 t. cinnamon
1 c. bite-size crispy corn cereal
    squares
1 c. bite-size crispy rice cereal
    squares
1 c. bite-size crispy wheat cereal
    squares
1 c. honey-nut doughnut-shaped
    oat cereal
3/4 c. sliced almonds, toasted
1/3 c. butter, melted
1 c. dried banana chips
1/2 c. dried blueberries or raisins

In a small bowl, mix sugar and cinnamon; set aside. In a large, microwave-safe bowl, combine cereals and melted butter; toss until evenly coated. Microwave, uncovered, on high for 2 minutes, stirring after one minute. Stir in sugar mixture and banana chips until evenly coated. Microwave, uncovered, for one additional minute. Spread on wax paper to cool. Transfer to an airtight container; stir in blueberries or raisins. Makes 12 to 14 servings.

Amanda Pennings
Walla Walla, WA

Cereal without the milk!
A big handful of this and
I'm out the door, ready to
start my day.

Melon-Berry Bowls

1 honeydew melon, halved and
  seeded
6-oz. container favorite-flavor
  yogurt
1/2 c. blueberries
1 c. granola cereal

Use a melon baller to scoop
honeydew into balls. Combine
melon balls with remaining
ingredients. Spoon into individual
bowls to serve. Serves 2 to 4.

23

**Jill Ball
Highland, UT**
I am always looking for
quick, healthy and yummy
breakfast ideas for my
teenagers. This one has
become a favorite!

Steak & Egg Breakfast Burrito

2 frozen sliced sandwich steaks
4 eggs
2 T. milk
2 t. fresh chives, chopped
salt and pepper to taste
2 corn tortillas
salsa to taste
1/2 c. shredded Mexican-blend
   cheese, divided

In a skillet over medium heat, cook steaks until no longer pink; drain and set aside. Beat together eggs, milk, chives, salt and pepper. In same skillet, scramble eggs to desired doneness. Divide eggs evenly between tortillas; top each with steak, salsa and cheese. Roll up and microwave on high setting for 20 to 30 seconds to melt cheese. Makes 2 servings.

Shelly Turner
Boise, ID
Such a great way to enjoy classic steak and eggs when you're in a hurry!

Fruited Orange Yogurt

8-oz. container mascarpone
   cheese
32-oz. container plain yogurt
1/3 c. sugar
juice and zest of 2 oranges
Garnish: granola, blueberries,
   raspberries, sliced bananas

In a bowl, combine cheese, yogurt
and sugar. Stir in juice and zest.
Sprinkle granola over top. Serve
with fresh fruit. Serves 4 to 6.

25

Beth Bennett
Stratham, NH
A smooth and crunchy, sweet
and zingy breakfast you can
enjoy on the go.

Pigs in the Clover

14-3/4 oz. can creamed corn
2 to 3 potatoes, peeled, boiled
   and cubed
salt and pepper to taste
8 pork breakfast sausage links,
   browned

Pour creamed corn into a greased
8"x8" baking pan. Place potatoes
over corn; sprinkle with salt and
pepper. Arrange sausage links on top.
Cover with aluminum foil. Bake at
350 degrees for 30 minutes, or until
bubbly. Serves 4 to 6.

Cathy Nign
Temple City, CA

My Norwegian mother-in-law
gave me this recipe. She
told me this was a dish
she ate while growing up.

Breakfast Pizza

11-oz. tube refrigerated
   thin-crust pizza dough
14-oz. can pizza sauce
16-oz. container ricotta cheese
1/4 c. fresh oregano, chopped
favorite pizza toppings
4 eggs
salt and pepper to taste

Roll out dough into a 13-inch by
9-inch rectangle; transfer to a
greased rimmed baking sheet.
Spread pizza sauce on dough,
leaving a 1/2-inch border. Top
with cheese, oregano and other
pizza toppings. Bake at 500 degrees
for 4 to 5 minutes, or until crust
begins to turn golden. Crack each
egg into a small bowl and slip onto
pizza, being careful not to break the
yolks. Bake for another 5 minutes,
until eggs are done as desired.
Serves 2 to 4.

27

Connie Hilty
Pearland, TX

Is there anything better
than pizza for breakfast?

Green Eggs & Ham

2 T. butter
1/2 c. fresh spinach
1 green onion, chopped
1/4 c. deli smoked ham, diced
3 eggs, beaten
2 T. pesto sauce
salt and pepper to taste

Melt butter in a skillet over medium heat. Cook spinach, green onion and ham in butter until warmed through and spinach is wilted, about 3 minutes. Add eggs to spinach mixture and cook until eggs start to set; stir in pesto, salt and pepper. Continue cooking until eggs reach desired doneness. Serves one to 2.

Chad Rutan
Gooseberry Patch

These are so good, I will eat them on a plane, on a train, on a boat, in a coat... anywhere, anytime!

PB&J Breakfast Bars

1-1/2 c. quick-cooking oats,
   uncooked
1/2 c. all-purpose flour
1/2 c. light brown sugar, packed
1/4 t. baking soda
1/4 t. plus 1/8 t. salt, divided
1/4 t. cinnamon
6 T. butter, melted
8-oz. pkg. cream cheese,
   softened
1/2 c. creamy peanut butter
1 egg, beaten
1/2 c. favorite-flavor jam

In a bowl, stir together oats, flour, brown sugar, baking soda, 1/4 teaspoon salt and cinnamon. Add melted butter and mix until crumbs form. Reserve 1/2 cup of oat mixture for topping; firmly spread remaining mixture in a lightly greased, parchment paper-lined 8"x8" baking pan. Bake at 350 degrees for 15 minutes, or until golden. In a bowl, beat together cream cheese, peanut butter, egg and remaining salt. Spread cream cheese mixture over baked crust; spread with jam. Top with reserved oat mixture. Bake for an additional 30 minutes, or until topping is golden; cool. Refrigerate for one hour, or until fully set. Cut into bars. Makes 12 to 15.

Angie Stewart Forester
Memphis, TN

This is our favorite quick breakfast item. My hubby can grab one of these as he walks out the door, because he always forgets to leave time for breakfast.

29

Lazy Man's Pancakes

3 T. butter
6 eggs
1-1/2 c. milk
1-1/2 c. all-purpose flour
3/4 t. salt
Optional: chopped walnuts,
  maple syrup

Melt butter in a 13"x9" baking pan
placed in a 425-degree oven.
Meanwhile, in a bowl, combine eggs,
milk, flour and salt; beat well. Slowly
pour mixture into buttered pan. Bake
at 425 degrees for 20 to 25 minutes,
until top is golden. Cut into squares;
serve topped with nuts and syrup,
if desired. Serves 5 to 6.

Mel Chencharick
Julian, PA

This is great when you're
pressed for time. No more
standing at the stove for an
hour flipping and frying...
just mix and pop in the oven.

Cranberry-Lime Cooler

6-oz. can frozen limeade
   concentrate, thawed
4 c. cold water
16-oz. bottle cranberry juice
   cocktail
1/4 c. orange drink mix
ice cubes
Garnish: fresh mint sprigs

Prepare limeade with water in a large
pitcher. Stir in cranberry juice and
orange drink mix. Pour over ice
cubes in tall mugs or glasses.
Garnish each with a sprig of mint.
Makes 8 servings.

31

Ellie Brandel
Milwaukie, OR
A refreshingly different
beverage to pair with
the rest of your
speedy breakfast.

Honey Crunch Granola

4 c. long-cooking oats, uncooked
1/2 c. unsalted slivered almonds
1/4 c. unsalted sunflower kernels
1/2 c. honey
1/2 c. butter
2 t. cinnamon
1/8 t. ground cloves
1 t. vanilla extract
1/8 t. salt

Mix oats, almonds and sunflower kernels in a large bowl; set aside. Combine honey, butter, spices, vanilla and salt in a microwave-safe bowl. Microwave on high setting until butter and honey are melted; stir well. Pour honey mixture over oat mixture; toss until well coated. Spread on a lightly greased 15"x10" jelly-roll pan. Bake at 350 degrees for 20 minutes, or until lightly golden. Allow to cool completely; store in an airtight container. Makes 8 servings.

Emily Hartzell
Portland, IN

For a delicious, healthy breakfast, serve over vanilla yogurt with fresh berries and bananas!

Sausage Muffins

1 lb. ground turkey sausage
1/4 c. butter
5-oz. jar sharp pasteurized
   process cheese spread
1/4 t. garlic powder
6 English muffins, split

In a skillet over medium heat, brown sausage; drain. Add butter, cheese and garlic powder; mix and cook until cheese melts. Spread sausage mixture on 6 English muffin halves. Place on an ungreased baking sheet and bake at 350 degrees for 15 minutes, or until heated through. Top with remaining halves of English muffins. Makes 6.

33

Carolyn Britton
Millry, AL

These are great to make ahead and freeze individually. Just heat and serve for a quick breakfast or snack.

Strawberry-Hazelnut Grits

3/4 c. quick-cooking grits,
   uncooked
1 T. butter
3 T. chocolate-hazelnut spread
6 to 7 strawberries, hulled and
   chopped

Prepare grits according to package
directions. Stir in butter and
chocolate-hazelnut spread. Fold in
strawberries. Serves 2.

Beth Kramer
Port Saint Lucie, FL

This combination of
strawberry, cocoa and
hazelnut is just too
yummy to pass up!

Barbara's Open-House Waffles

3 c. biscuit baking mix
1 c. millet flour
1/8 t. baking soda
1/4 c. canola oil
3 eggs, beaten
3 c. buttermilk
2 T. water
Garnish: maple syrup, fresh
   strawberries, whipped cream

In a bowl, whisk together baking mix,
flour and baking soda. Add remaining
ingredients except garnish and mix
well. Drop batter by 1/2 cupfuls onto
a heated waffle iron; cook according
to manufacturer's directions. Top
with maple syrup, strawberries and
whipped cream. Serves 6 to 8.

35

Barbara McCurry
Carpinteria, CA

Every Saturday morning,
I serve these for family &
friends...it's fun, and the
neighbors love it!

Apple Breakfast Cobbler

4 apples, peeled, cored and
  sliced
1/4 c. honey
1 t. cinnamon
2 T. butter, melted
2 c. granola cereal
Garnish: milk or cream

Place apples in a slow cooker sprayed
with non-stick vegetable spray. In a
bowl, combine remaining ingredients
except garnish; sprinkle over apples.
Cover and cook on low setting for
7 to 9 hours, or on high setting for
3 to 4 hours. Garnish with milk or
cream. Serves 4.

Debi Gilpin
Sharpsburg, GA
What a fabulous slow-cooker
treat to wake up to on a
chilly winter morning!

Cranberry Hootycreek Pancakes

1/2 c. all-purpose flour
1/2 c. quick-cooking oats,
   uncooked
1 T. sugar
1 t. baking powder
1/2 t. baking soda
1/2 t. salt
1 t. vanilla extract
3/4 c. buttermilk
2 T. oil
1 egg, beaten
1/2 c. white chocolate chips
1/2 c. sweetened dried
   cranberries

37

In a bowl, mix flour, oats, sugar,
baking powder, baking soda and salt.
Add vanilla, buttermilk, oil and egg;
stir until well blended. Stir in white
chocolate chips and cranberries.
In a large, lightly greased griddle
over medium heat, drop batter by
1/4 cupfuls. Cook for about
3 minutes, until tops start to form
bubbles. Flip and cook 2 additional
minutes, or until both sides are
golden. Serves 4.

Sarah Lundvall
Ephrata, PA

This is my take on a
favorite cookie recipe...
for breakfast. My 2-year-old
gobbles them up faster
than I can make them.

Melt-In-Your-Mouth Biscuits

1-1/2 c. all-purpose flour
1/2 c. whole-wheat flour
4 t. baking powder
1/2 t. salt
2 T. sugar
1/4 c. chilled butter, sliced
1/4 c. shortening
2/3 c. milk
1 egg, beaten

In a large bowl, sift flours, baking powder, salt and sugar together; cut in butter and shortening. Add milk; stir in egg. Knead on a floured surface until smooth; roll out to 1/2-inch thickness. Cut with a biscuit cutter; place biscuits on ungreased baking sheets. Bake at 450 degrees for 10 to 15 minutes, until golden. Makes one to 2 dozen.

Sherri Hagel
Spokane, WA

Split and served with butter and jam or topped with sausage gravy, these flaky biscuits live up to their name!

Sausage Gravy

1 lb. ground pork breakfast
  sausage
1/4 c. all-purpose flour
3 to 4 c. milk
1/2 t. salt
1/4 t. pepper

Brown sausage in a large skillet over
medium-high heat; do not drain.
Stir in flour until mixture becomes
thick. Reduce heat to medium-low.
Gradually add milk, stirring
constantly, until mixture reaches
desired thickness. Season with salt
and pepper. Serves 4 to 6.

Leslie Stimel
Columbus, OH

It's a snap to make this
delicious homestyle gravy.

Bacon Griddle Cakes

12 slices bacon
2 c. pancake mix
Garnish: butter, maple syrup

On a griddle set to medium heat, cook bacon until crisp. Drain, reserving 2 tablespoons drippings. Meanwhile, prepare pancake mix according to package directions, omitting a little of the water or milk for a thicker batter. Arrange bacon slices 2 inches apart on griddle greased with reserved drippings. Slowly pour pancake batter over each piece of bacon, covering each slice. Cook until golden on both sides; serve with butter and maple syrup. Serves 4 to 6.

Joseph Drushal
Chicago, IL
So simple but so delicious! Why didn't I think of this sooner?

Bacon & Egg Potato Skins

2 baking potatoes
4 eggs, beaten
1 to 2 t. butter
salt and pepper to taste
1/4 c. shredded Monterey Jack
  cheese
1/4 c. shredded Cheddar cheese
4 slices bacon, crisply cooked
  and crumbled
Garnish: sour cream, chopped
  fresh chives

43

Bake potatoes at 400 degrees for one hour, until tender. Slice potatoes in half lengthwise; scoop out centers and reserve for another recipe. Place potato skins on a lightly greased baking sheet. Bake at 400 degrees for 6 to 8 minutes, until crisp. In a skillet over medium heat, scramble eggs in butter just until they begin to set. Add salt and pepper; remove from heat. Spoon equal amounts of eggs, cheeses and bacon into each potato skin. Reduce heat to 350 degrees and bake for 7 to 10 minutes, until cheese is melted and eggs are completely set. Garnish with sour cream and chives. Makes 4 servings.

Dale Duncan
Waterloo, IA

A tummy-filling
complete meal in a
potato skin...yummy!

Luscious Blueberry Syrup

1/2 c. sugar
1 T. cornstarch
1/3 c. water
2 c. fresh or frozen blueberries

In a saucepan over medium heat, combine sugar and cornstarch. Stir in water gradually. Add berries; bring to a boil. Boil, stirring constantly, for one minute, or until mixture thickens. Serve warm, or pour into a covered jar and keep in the refrigerator for several days. Makes about 2-1/2 cups.

Cindy Williams
Owensboro, KY
So quick & easy! It's delicious drizzled warm or cold over waffles, pancakes and even over ice cream or a slice of pound cake.

Blueberry-Lemon Crepes

3-oz. pkg. cream cheese,
    softened
1-1/2 c. half-and-half
1 T. lemon juice
3-3/4 pkg. instant lemon
    pudding mix
1/2 c. biscuit baking mix
1 egg
6 T. milk
1 c. blueberry pie filling

Combine cream cheese, half-and-half, lemon juice and dry pudding mix in a bowl. Beat with an electric mixer on low speed for 2 minutes. Refrigerate for 30 minutes. Lightly grease a 6" skillet and place over medium-high heat. In a bowl, combine biscuit baking mix, egg and milk. Beat until smooth. Pour 2 tablespoons of batter into skillet for each crepe. Rotating the skillet quickly, allow batter to cover the bottom of the skillet. Cook each crepe until lightly golden, then flip, cooking again until just golden. Spoon 2 tablespoonfuls of cream cheese mixture onto each crepe and roll up. Top with remaining cream cheese mixture and pie filling. Makes 6 servings.

45

Jo Ann

A scrumptious and refreshing breakfast!

After-Church Egg Muffins

10-3/4 oz. can Cheddar cheese
 soup
1-1/2 c. milk
4 eggs
4 English muffins, split and
 toasted
3 T. butter, divided
4 slices Canadian bacon

In a bowl, mix together soup and milk. Fill 4 greased custard cups 1/4 full with soup mixture. Set cups on a baking sheet. Crack an egg into each cup, being careful not to break the yolks. Bake cups at 350 degrees for 12 minutes. Meanwhile, brown both sides of bacon in a skillet over medium heat. Top each muffin half with one teaspoon butter. Place 4 muffin halves on a baking sheet. Top each with a slice of bacon. Turn out a baked egg onto each bacon-topped muffin half. Drizzle remaining cheese sauce over each egg. Top with other halves of muffins. Bake for an additional 2 minutes, or until heated through. Makes 4 servings.

Megan Brooks
Antioch, TN
I whip these up for my boys almost every Sunday after church...they start asking for them right when we walk in the door.

Chocolate Chip-Pumpkin Waffles

1 egg, beaten
3/4 c. canned pumpkin
1/4 c. brown sugar, packed
1/4 c. butter, melted and slightly
  cooled
1-3/4 c. milk
1-1/2 c. all-purpose flour
1/2 c. whole-wheat flour
1 T. flax meal
1-1/2 t. pumpkin pie spice
1 T. baking powder
1/2 t. salt
1/2 c. semi-sweet chocolate chips
Optional: vanilla yogurt,
  cinnamon-sugar, toasted
  pumpkin seeds

47

In a bowl, whisk together egg,
pumpkin, brown sugar, butter and
milk. Add dry ingredients; whisk
well until smooth. Fold in chocolate
chips. Pour batter by 1/2 cupfuls into
a greased hot waffle iron. Cook
waffles according to manufacturer's
directions. Top waffles with a dollop
of yogurt, cinnamon-sugar and
pumpkin seeds, if desired. Serves 4.

Cindy Jamieson
Barrie, Ontario
These taste wonderful,
and the kids are none
the wiser that they are
a tad healthier!

Sugarplum Bacon

1/2 c. brown sugar, packed
1 t. cinnamon
1/2 lb. bacon

In a bowl, combine brown sugar and cinnamon. Cut each bacon slice in half crosswise; dredge each slice in brown sugar mixture. Twist bacon slices and place in an ungreased 13"x9" baking pan. Bake at 350 degrees for 15 to 20 minutes, until bacon is crisp and sugar is bubbly. Place bacon on aluminum foil to cool. Serve at room temperature. Makes 8 servings.

Beth Burgmeier
East Dubuque, IL

Crunchy, sweet and salty... this bacon is out-of-this-world good! Cook some up for your brunch guests. They're sure to love it.

Farmers' Market Omelet

1 t. olive oil
1 slice bacon, diced
2 T. onion, chopped
2 T. zucchini, diced
5 cherry tomatoes, quartered
1/2 t. fresh thyme, minced
3 eggs, beaten
1/4 c. fontina cheese, shredded

Heat oil in a skillet over medium-high heat. Add bacon and onion; cook and stir until bacon is crisp and onion is tender. Add zucchini, tomatoes and thyme. Allow to cook until zucchini is soft and juice from tomatoes has slightly evaporated. Lower heat to medium and stir in eggs. Cook, lifting edges to allow uncooked egg to flow underneath. When eggs are almost fully cooked, sprinkle with cheese and fold over. Serves one.

49

Vickie

I love visiting the farmers' market bright & early on Saturday mornings... a terrific way to begin the day!

Scrambled Eggs & Lox

6 eggs, beaten
1 T. fresh dill, minced
1 T. fresh chives, minced
1 T. green onion, minced
pepper to taste
2 T. butter
4-oz. pkg. smoked salmon, diced

Whisk together eggs, herbs, onion and pepper. Melt butter in a large skillet over medium heat. Add egg mixture and stir gently with a spatula until eggs begin to set. Stir in salmon; continue cooking until eggs reach desired doneness. Serves 3.

Jackie Smulski
Lyons, IL

These eggs are sure to please everyone...they're excellent with toasted English muffins or bagels.

Orange-Cinnamon French Toast

2 to 4 T. butter, melted
2 T. honey
1/2 t. cinnamon
3 eggs, beaten
1/2 c. frozen orange juice
    concentrate, partially thawed
1/8 t. salt
6 slices French bread

Combine butter, honey and
cinnamon together in a
13"x9" baking pan and set aside.
Blend eggs, orange juice and salt
together. Dip bread slices into egg
mixture, coating both sides.
Arrange dipped bread slices in
baking pan. Bake, uncovered, at
400 degrees for 15 to 20 minutes,
until golden. Serves 3 to 4.

51

Debra Fleischacker
Aurora, CO
Good recipes always get
passed along, as this
one will!

Eggs Benedict

8 slices Canadian bacon
1 t. lemon juice or vinegar
8 eggs
4 English muffins, split and
   toasted
3 T. butter, softened and divided
1 c. Hollandaise sauce, divided
3 T. fresh chives, chopped

Brown bacon in a skillet over medium heat. Meanwhile, fill a large saucepan with 2 inches of water and lemon juice or vinegar; bring to a simmer. Crack each egg into a shallow bowl and slip them, one at a time, into the water. Poach for about 3 minutes, until whites are set and yolks are soft. Remove eggs with a slotted spoon and drain on paper towels. Top each toasted muffin half with one teaspoon butter, one slice of bacon, one egg and a drizzle of Hollandaise sauce. Sprinkle with chives. Serves 4.

Diana Chaney
Olathe, KS

Who knew a dish that looks this elegant would be so easy? Nothing beats these eggs paired with a warm cup of tea.

Spinach & Tomato French Toast

3 eggs
salt and pepper to taste
8 slices Italian bread
4 c. fresh spinach, torn
2 tomatoes, sliced
Garnish: grated Parmesan cheese

In a bowl, beat eggs with salt and pepper. Dip bread slices into egg. Place in a lightly greased skillet over medium heat; cook one side until lightly golden. Place fresh spinach and two slices of tomato onto each slice, pressing lightly to secure. Flip and briefly cook on other side until golden. Serves 4.

53

Linda Bonwill
Englewood, FL

A healthier way to make French toast...plus, it looks so pretty!

Granny Ruth's Chocolate Gravy

1 c. sugar
2 t. baking cocoa
1 t. cornstarch
1/2 c. milk
1 t. butter
1 t. vanilla extract

Mix together all ingredients in a saucepan over medium heat. Cook and stir until mixture reaches desired thickness. Serve warm. Makes about 6 servings.

Julie Marsh
Shelbyville, TN

This recipe is so special to our family...Granny Ruth made this for everyone. It is wonderful over hot biscuits!

Red Velvet Pancakes

1-1/2 c. all-purpose flour
2 T. baking cocoa
4 t. sugar
1-1/2 t. baking powder
1/2 t. baking soda
1 t. cinnamon
1 t. salt
2 eggs
1-1/4 c. buttermilk
1 T. red food coloring
1-1/2 t. vanilla extract
1/4 c. butter, melted
Optional: maple syrup, butter,
    whipped cream cheese

In a bowl, whisk together all dry
ingredients. In a separate bowl, mix
eggs, buttermilk, food coloring and
vanilla. Add to dry ingredients and
mix well. Fold in melted butter.
Using an ice cream scoop, drop
batter onto a lightly greased, hot
griddle and cook until edges darken,
about 5 minutes. Flip and cook until
done. Serve topped with syrup and
butter or whipped cream cheese.
Makes one dozen pancakes.

Ashlee Haefs
Buna, TX

Red velvet cake is one of my
family's favorites, so with
this recipe we can have it
for breakfast...what a great
way to start the day!

55

Yummy Sausage Cups

1 lb. maple-flavored ground
    pork breakfast sausage
8-oz. pkg. shredded sharp
    Cheddar cheese
16-oz. container sour cream
1-oz. pkg. ranch salad dressing
    mix
4 2.1-oz. pkgs. frozen phyllo
    cups

Brown sausage in a skillet over
medium heat; drain and return to
skillet. Stir in remaining ingredients
except phyllo cups. Fill each phyllo
cup with a scoop of sausage mixture.
Arrange cups on ungreased baking
sheets. Bake at 350 degrees for
15 minutes, or until heated through
and cups are golden. Makes 5 dozen.

Angie Walsh
Cedar Rapids, IA
We enjoy having these
on Christmas day, but they're
good any time of year!
My mother-in-law makes them,
and they are a huge hit!

Sausage & Red Pepper Strata

6-oz. pkg. ground pork sausage
1/2 t. dried oregano
1/4 t. red pepper flakes
4 slices French bread, cubed
1/2 red pepper, diced
1 t. dried parsley
4 eggs
1 c. evaporated milk
1 t. Dijon mustard
1/4 t. pepper
1/2 c. shredded sharp Cheddar
   cheese

57

Brown sausage with oregano and red pepper flakes in a skillet over medium heat; drain and set aside. Line the bottom of a greased 8"x8" baking pan with bread; top with sausage mixture, red pepper and parsley. Set aside. Whisk together eggs, milk, mustard and pepper. Pour evenly over sausage mixture; cover tightly with aluminum foil and refrigerate 8 hours to overnight. Bake, covered with aluminum foil, at 350 degrees for 55 minutes. Remove foil; sprinkle with cheese and bake for an additional 5 minutes, or until cheese is melted. Serves 4 to 6.

Lynette Mull
Newton, KS

A delicious layered casserole you make the night before.

Sausage-Mozzarella Loaves

2 16-oz. loaves frozen bread
   dough, thawed
1 lb. ground pork sausage,
   browned and drained
12-oz. pkg. shredded mozzarella
   cheese
2 eggs, beaten
grated Parmesan cheese to taste

Roll bread loaves into two 16-inch by
8-inch rectangles. Sprinkle sausage
and mozzarella cheese over each
rectangle. Drizzle beaten eggs over
top. Top with Parmesan cheese. Roll
up each rectangle jelly-roll style,
starting at a short end. Place rolls
into 2 greased 9"x5" loaf pans,
seam-side down. Bake at 400 degrees
for 30 to 40 minutes, until tops are
golden. Serve warm. Makes 2 loaves.

Karen Carr
Elkins, WV

Golden bread loaves
filled with cheese and
sausage...yummy!

Puffy Pear Pancake

3 eggs, beaten
1 c. milk
1 t. vanilla extract
1 c. all-purpose flour
3 T. sugar
1/4 t. salt
4 pears, cored, peeled and sliced
1/4 c. brown sugar, packed
1/4 c. lemon juice

In a large bowl, whisk together eggs and milk. Add vanilla, flour, sugar and salt; whisk to combine. Pour batter into a large, ungreased oven-proof skillet. Bake at 425 degrees until golden and puffy, about 25 minutes. Meanwhile, combine pears, brown sugar and lemon juice in a bowl; stir well. Pour into a skillet over medium heat; sauté until pears are golden, about 5 minutes. Remove from heat. Spoon warm pear mixture over pancake before serving. Cut into wedges. Serves 4.

59

Jo Ann

Top each slice with a sprinkling of powdered sugar...yum!

Make-Ahead Breakfast Eggs

1 doz. eggs
1/2 c. milk
1/2 t. salt
1/4 t. pepper
1 T. butter
1 c. sour cream
12 slices bacon, crisply cooked
  and crumbled
1 c. shredded sharp Cheddar
  cheese

Beat together eggs, milk, salt and pepper; set aside. In a large skillet, melt butter over medium-low heat. Add egg mixture, stirring occasionally until eggs are set but still moist; remove from heat and cool. Stir in sour cream. Spread mixture in a greased shallow 2-quart casserole dish; top with bacon and cheese. Cover dish and refrigerate overnight. Uncover and bake at 300 degrees for 15 to 20 minutes, until heated through and cheese is melted. Serves 6 to 8.

Tamara Wallace
Roscoe, IL

For a wedding shower, my mom created a family cookbook... she asked everyone for special recipes and memories. This dish comes from that treasured collection.

Quick Strawberry Cream Danish

2 8-oz. pkgs. cream cheese,
    softened
1 egg, separated
1 t. vanilla extract
1 t. lemon juice
1 T. all-purpose flour
2 8-oz. tubes refrigerated
    crescent rolls
1/2 c. strawberry preserves,
    divided

Beat together cream cheese, egg
yolk, vanilla, lemon juice and flour.
Unroll and separate rolls; place a
teaspoon of cream cheese mixture
in the center of each triangle. Fold
over edges of rolls, leaving center
open. Brush with beaten egg white.
Place on ungreased baking sheets.
Bake at 350 degrees for 20 minutes.
Remove from oven and cool slightly.
Top each with a teaspoon of
strawberry preserves. Makes 16.

61

Beth Bundy
Long Prairie, MN

These are super easy, super
tasty and super pretty. A
couple of these with your
coffee will definitely make
your morning bright!

French Toast Casserole

1 c. brown sugar, packed
1/2 c. butter
2 c. corn syrup
1 loaf French bread, sliced
5 eggs, beaten
1-1/2 c. milk
1 t. vanilla extract
Garnish: powdered sugar,
  maple syrup

Melt together brown sugar, butter and corn syrup in a saucepan over low heat; pour into a greased 13"x9" baking pan. Arrange bread slices over mixture and set aside. Whisk together eggs, milk and vanilla; pour over bread, coating all slices. Cover and refrigerate overnight. Uncover and bake at 350 degrees for 30 minutes, or until lightly golden. Sprinkle with powdered sugar; serve with warm syrup. Makes 6 to 8 servings.

Lori Hurley
Fishers, IN

A really simple way to make French toast for a crowd. Pop it in the fridge the night before, then all you have to do is bake it in the morning!

Grandma's Warm Breakfast Fruit

3 apples, peeled, cored and
   thickly sliced
1 orange, peeled and sectioned
3/4 c. raisins
1/2 c. dried plums, chopped
3 c. plus 3 T. water, divided
1/2 c. sugar
1/2 t. cinnamon
2 T. cornstarch
Garnish: granola

Combine fruit and 3 cups water in
a saucepan over medium heat. Bring
to a boil; reduce heat and simmer
for 10 minutes. Stir in sugar and
cinnamon. In a small bowl, mix
together cornstarch and remaining
water; stir into fruit mixture. Bring
to a boil, stirring constantly; cook
and stir for 2 minutes. Spoon into
bowls; top with granola to serve.
Serves 6 to 8.

63

Virginia Watson
Scranton, PA
Keep this warm for brunch
in a mini slow cooker.

Best Brunch Casserole

Lita Hardy
Santa Cruz, CA
My family & friends have been enjoying this dish for over 30 years!

4 c. croutons
2 c. shredded Cheddar cheese
8 eggs, beaten
4 c. milk
1 t. salt
1 t. pepper
2 t. mustard
1 T. dried, minced onion
6 slices bacon, crisply cooked
   and crumbled

Spread croutons in a greased
13"x9" baking pan; sprinkle with
cheese and set aside. In a bowl, whisk
together remaining ingredients
except bacon; pour over cheese.
Sprinkle bacon on top. Bake,
uncovered, at 325 degrees for 55 to
60 minutes, until set. Serves 8.

Best-Ever Brunch Potatoes

2-1/2 lbs. redskin potatoes, diced
3 T. olive oil
8 eggs, beaten
1 t. salt
1/2 T. pepper
8 slices bacon, crisply cooked
   and crumbled
3/4 c. French onion dip
3/4 c. shredded sharp Cheddar
   cheese
1/2 c. green onions, chopped

In a skillet over medium heat, fry potatoes in oil until tender. In a separate lightly greased skillet, scramble eggs until fluffy; season with salt and pepper. Fold bacon, dip and cheese into potatoes; stir in scrambled eggs. Sprinkle green onions over top. Serves 6 to 8.

65

Gaybrielle Ray
Springfield, OH

I created this recipe by tossing together several of my favorite ingredients... it was a hit!

Sweet & Easy Iced Coffee

1/2 c. sweetened condensed milk,
  divided
4 c. strong brewed coffee, cooled
ice cubes

Place 2 tablespoons of sweetened
condensed milk into each of 4 tall
glasses. Pour one cup of cooled coffee
into each glass; stir to combine. Fill
glasses with ice; stir to chill. Serves 4.

Jen Licon-Conner
Gooseberry Patch

My love of iced coffee
started one summer when it
was just too hot for my
morning cup...now I make
it all year 'round!

Blueberry Pillows

8-oz. pkg. cream cheese,
  softened
16 slices Italian bread
1/2 c. blueberries
2 eggs, beaten
1/2 c. milk
1 t. vanilla extract

Spread cream cheese evenly on
8 bread slices; arrange blueberries
in a single layer over cream cheese.
Top with remaining bread slices,
gently pressing to seal; set aside.
Whisk together eggs, milk and vanilla
in a small bowl; brush over bread
slices. Arrange on a greased hot
griddle; cook until golden. Flip
and cook other side until golden.
Serves 8.

67

Kristie Rigo
Friedens, PA
A delightful blend of cream
cheese and blueberries
stuffed inside French toast.

Hashbrown Quiche

3 c. frozen shredded
  hashbrowns, thawed
1/4 c. butter, melted
3 eggs, beaten
1 c. half-and-half
3/4 c. cooked ham, diced
1/2 c. green onions, chopped
1 c. shredded Cheddar cheese
salt and pepper to taste

In an ungreased 9" pie plate,
combine hashbrowns and butter.
Press hashbrowns into the bottom
and up the sides of the pie plate. Bake
at 450 degrees for 20 to 25 minutes
until, golden and crisp. Remove
from oven and cool slightly.
Meanwhile, combine remaining
ingredients in a bowl. Pour mixture
over hashbrowns. Lower oven
temperature to 350 degrees; bake
for 30 minutes, or until quiche is
golden and set. Serves 4 to 6.

Sonya Labbe
Santa Monica, CA

The crust of this quiche is
made with frozen hashbrowns.
It is always a hit at family
potlucks and brunches.

Dilled Crab Egg Cups

1/2 lb. crabmeat, flaked
8-oz. pkg. cream cheese, diced
1 T. fresh dill, chopped and
   divided
1 doz. eggs
1/2 c. milk
1/2 c. sour cream
Optional: salad greens, favorite-
   flavor salad dressing

Divide crabmeat and cream cheese
evenly among 12 greased muffin cups.
Sprinkle dill into each cup. In a
bowl, whisk together eggs, milk and
sour cream. Divide egg mixture
among muffin cups, filling each
about 3/4 full. Bake at 450 degrees
for 10 to 15 minutes, until puffed and
golden. Cool slightly; remove from
tin. Serve egg cups on a bed of salad
greens drizzled with dressing, if
desired. Makes one dozen.

69

Sandra Sullivan
Aurora, CO

A great dish for
pop-up brunches and
get-togethers.

Fiesta Corn Tortilla Quiche

1 lb. hot ground pork sausage
5 6-inch corn tortillas
4-oz. can chopped green chiles,
    drained
1 c. shredded Cheddar cheese
1 c. shredded Monterey Jack
    cheese
6 eggs, beaten
1/2 c. whipping cream
1/2 c. small-curd cottage cheese

Brown sausage in a skillet over medium heat; drain. Meanwhile, arrange tortillas in a lightly greased 9" pie plate, overlapping on the bottom and extending 1/2 inch over the edge of plate. Spoon sausage, chiles and cheeses into tortilla-lined pie plate. In a bowl, beat together remaining ingredients. Pour egg mixture over sausage mixture. Bake, uncovered, at 375 degrees for 45 minutes, or until golden. Cut into wedges to serve. Serves 4.

Vickie

I love that the crust of this quiche is made out of tortillas. Plus, it has a great spicy flavor, perfect for chilly mornings.

Breezy Brunch Skillet

6 slices bacon, diced
6 c. frozen diced potatoes
3/4 c. green pepper, chopped
1/2 c. onion, chopped
1 t. salt
1/4 t. pepper
6 eggs
1/2 c. shredded Cheddar cheese

In a large skillet over medium heat, cook bacon until crisp. Drain and set aside, reserving 2 T. drippings. In the same skillet, add potatoes, green pepper, onion, salt and pepper to drippings. Cook and stir for 2 minutes. Cover and cook for about 15 minutes, stirring occasionally, until potatoes are golden and tender. With a spoon, make 6 wells in potato mixture. Crack one egg into each well, taking care not to break the yolks. Cover and cook on low heat for 8 to 10 minutes, until eggs are completely set. Sprinkle with cheese and bacon. Serves 4 to 6.

71

Jill Ross
Gooseberry Patch

This one-skillet meal is a snap to toss together and the results are scrumptious. I'll even cook this up for dinner, it's so good!

Apple Walnut Coffee Cake

3 eggs, beaten
1 c. oil
2 c. sugar
1 T. vanilla extract
3 c. all-purpose flour
1 t. salt
1/2 t. baking powder
1 t. baking soda
3/4 t. nutmeg
1 T. cinnamon
2 c. apples, peeled, cored and
　　chopped
1 c. chopped walnuts

In a bowl, combine all ingredients except apple and nuts; mix well. Stir in apple and nuts; pour into greased and floured Bundt® pan. Bake at 300 degrees for 45 minutes. Increase heat to 325 degrees and bake an additional 20 minutes. Cool on a wire rack for 20 minutes; turn out onto a serving plate. Top with Glaze before serving. Serves 16.

Glaze:

1 c. powdered sugar
1-1/2 T. milk
1/2 t. vanilla

In a bowl, whisk together all ingredients.

Patty Sandness
Eastford, CT
The chopped apple and walnuts really set this coffee cake apart. It has all the yummy flavors of apple pie, but in a cake!

Cranberry-Orange Warmer ▶️

16-oz. pkg. frozen cranberries, thawed
4-inch cinnamon stick
8 c. water
6-oz. can frozen orange juice concentrate, thawed
6-oz. can frozen lemonade concentrate, thawed
1 c. sugar

In a saucepan, bring cranberries, cinnamon stick and water to a boil. Boil for 5 minutes. Strain, discarding cranberries and cinnamon stick. Return juice to saucepan. Add juice concentrates and sugar to saucepan; stir until sugar melts. Serve warm. Makes 20 servings.

73

Della Feist
Faith, SD
This is a favorite drink around our home during the fall and winter holidays. Make a double batch and invite friends over.

Sausage-Cranberry Quiche

1/2 lb. sage-flavored ground
   pork sausage
1/4 c. onion, chopped
3/4 c. sweetened dried
   cranberries
9-inch pie crust
1-1/2 c. shredded Monterey Jack
   cheese
3 eggs, beaten
1-1/2 c. half-and-half

In a large skillet over medium-high heat, brown sausage with onion; drain. Remove from heat and stir in cranberries. Line a 9" pie plate with pie crust. Sprinkle cheese into crust; evenly spoon in sausage mixture. In a bowl, combine eggs and half-and-half; whisk until mixed but not frothy. Pour egg mixture over sausage mixture. Bake at 375 degrees for 40 to 45 minutes, until a knife inserted in the center comes out clean. Let stand for 10 minutes before serving. Makes 6 servings.

Wanda Closs
Mount Airy, MD
The tartness of cranberries combined with spicy sausage makes a terrific match!

Pennsylvania Dutch Scrapple

1 lb. boneless pork loin, chopped
1 c. cornmeal
14-1/2 oz. can chicken broth
1/4 t. dried thyme
1/4 t. salt
1/2 c. all-purpose flour
1/4 t. pepper
2 T. oil
Optional: maple syrup

In a saucepan, cover pork with water; bring to a boil over medium heat. Simmer until fork-tender, about an hour; drain. Process in a food processor until minced. In a large saucepan over medium heat, combine pork, cornmeal, broth, thyme and salt; bring to a boil. Reduce heat and simmer, stirring constantly, for 2 minutes, or until mixture is very thick. Line a 9"x5" loaf pan with wax paper, letting paper extend above top of pan. Spoon pork mixture into pan; cover and chill for 4 hours to overnight. Unmold; cut into slices and set aside. On a plate, combine flour and pepper. Coat slices with flour mixture. In a large skillet, heat oil over medium heat; cook slices on both sides until golden. Drizzle with syrup, if desired. Serves 12.

75

Virginia Watson
Scranton, PA
Squares of this savory dish are usually served for breakfast...but sometimes, it's great for dinner too.

Cathy's Scotch Eggs

1 lb. ground pork sausage
2 T. dried parsley
1/2 t. dried sage
1/2 t. dried thyme
8 eggs, hard-boiled and peeled
1/2 c. all-purpose flour
1/2 t. salt
1/4 t. pepper
2 eggs, lightly beaten
1-1/2 c. dry bread crumbs
oil for frying
Optional: mustard

Combine sausage and herbs; mix well. Divide into 8 patties. Cover each hard-boiled egg with a sausage patty, pressing to cover and seal. Combine flour, salt and pepper. Roll eggs in flour mixture, then in beaten eggs and bread crumbs. Heat one inch of oil in a saucepan over medium-high heat. Cook eggs, a few at a time, in hot oil for 10 minutes, or until golden on all sides. Drain; chill in refrigerator. Slice into halves or quarters. Serve chilled with mustard, if desired. Serves 8.

Jamie Wyatt
Fayetteville, GA
My husband and I fell in love with Scotch Eggs while visiting England in 1980. Upon our return, my cousin shared her family recipe with us!

Southern Veggie Brunch Casserole

1 lb. ground pork sausage,
  browned and drained
1/2 c. green onions, chopped
1 green pepper, diced
1 red pepper, diced
1 jalapeño pepper, seeded and
  diced
2 tomatoes, chopped
2 c. shredded mozzarella cheese
1 c. biscuit baking mix
1 doz. eggs, beaten
1 c. milk
1/2 t. dried oregano
1/2 t. salt
1/4 t. pepper

77

In a greased 3-quart casserole dish, layer sausage, onions, peppers, tomatoes and cheese. In a large bowl, whisk together remaining ingredients; pour over cheese. Bake, uncovered, at 350 degrees for 55 to 60 minutes, until set and top is golden. Let stand for 10 minutes before serving. Serves 6 to 8.

Jennifer McClure
Lebanon, IN
Our family always has this breakfast dish for dinner, and it's fondly called "brinner" by our two children.

Country Cabin Potatoes

4 14-1/2 oz. cans sliced potatoes,
    drained
2 10-3/4 oz. cans cream of
    celery soup
16-oz. container sour cream
10 slices bacon, crisply cooked
    and crumbled
6 green onions, thinly sliced

Place potatoes in a slow cooker. In
a bowl, combine remaining
ingredients; pour over potatoes and
stir gently. Cover and cook on high
setting for 4 to 5 hours. Makes 10 to
12 servings.

Carol Lytle
Columbus, OH

One fall, we stayed in a
beautiful 1800s log cabin in
southern Ohio. Not only was
it peaceful and relaxing, but
breakfast was brought to us
each morning...what a treat!

Sausage Breakfast Bake

1 lb. hot ground pork sausage
28-oz. pkg. frozen hashbrowns
   with onions and peppers,
   thawed
1 c. sliced mushrooms
2 c. shredded Monterey Jack
   cheese
10 eggs
1/2 c. milk
salt and pepper to taste

In a skillet over medium heat, brown
sausage; drain. In a large bowl,
combine sausage, hashbrowns,
mushrooms and cheese. Spread
evenly in a greased 13"x9" baking
pan. Beat together eggs, milk, salt
and pepper. Pour egg mixture
over hashbrown mixture. Cover
with aluminum foil and bake at
375 degrees for one hour. Remove
foil and continue baking for an
additional 15 minutes, or until
golden. Serves 8.

79

Roxanne Sulzbach
Akron, OH
This tasty bake can be made
ahead and warmed for a quick
breakfast...my husband
and son love it!

Tex-Mex Egg Puff

1 doz. eggs, beaten
2 4-oz. cans chopped green
   chiles, drained
1/2 c. butter, melted and cooled
   slightly
1/2 c. all-purpose flour
1 t. baking powder
1/2 t. salt
16-oz. pkg. shredded Monterey
   Jack cheese
16-oz. container small-curd
   cottage cheese

In a large bowl, whisk together all ingredients. Spoon into a greased 13"x9" baking pan. Bake, uncovered, at 350 degrees for 35 to 40 minutes, until set. Cut into squares. Serves 8 to 10.

Carol Creed
Battlefield, MO
I experimented with the
ingredients until this recipe
was just right! Mix, bake
and serve. How easy is that?

Mom's Cheesy Hashbrowns

1/4 c. butter
1 sweet onion, chopped
2 c. shredded Cheddar cheese
1 c. sour cream
30-oz. pkg. frozen country-style
   shredded hashbrowns, thawed

Melt butter in a saucepan over medium heat. Add onion and cook until translucent, about 5 minutes. Mix in cheese and continue stirring until melted. Remove from heat; stir in sour cream. Gently fold mixture into hashbrowns. Spoon into a greased 2-quart casserole dish. Bake, uncovered, at 350 degrees for 60 to 75 minutes, until heated through and top is golden. Serves 6 to 8.

81

Valerie Hendrickson
Cedar Springs, MI

My mother used to make this scrumptious dish the old-fashioned way. My version is simplified, yet is still full of hearty homestyle flavor!

Easy Breakfast Squares

24-oz. pkg. frozen shredded
   hashbrowns
1-1/2 c. shredded mozzarella
   cheese
1-1/2 c. shredded Cheddar
   cheese
1 onion, diced
2 c. cooked ham, diced
salt and pepper to taste
3 eggs
1 c. milk

In a lightly greased 13"x9" baking pan,
layer hashbrowns, cheeses, onion and
ham; season with salt and pepper. Set
aside. In a bowl, beat together eggs
and milk; pour over ham. Cover;
refrigerate 8 hours to overnight.
Uncover; bake at 350 degrees for
45 minutes. Cut into squares to
serve. Serves 6 to 8.

Vicki Hirsch
Platteville, WI

This overnight dish is
filled with all your
breakfast favorites!

Mexican Brunch Casserole

2 4-oz. cans whole green chiles,
  drained
2 to 3 tomatoes, chopped
2 c. shredded Colby Jack cheese
1 c. biscuit baking mix
3 eggs
1 c. milk
1/2 t. salt

In a lightly greased 8"x8" baking pan,
layer chiles, tomatoes and cheese.
Beat together remaining ingredients
and spoon over cheese. Bake,
uncovered, at 375 degrees for 30 to
35 minutes, until set. Serves 3 to 4.

83

Olive Herzberg
Lomita, CA

This is a great brunch
dish...it's got yummy
Mexican flavors that are
sure to have you coming
back for seconds.

Mushroom & Sausage Mini Quiches

8-oz. pkg. breakfast turkey
   sausage links, sliced
1 t. olive oil
8-oz. can sliced mushrooms
1/4 c. green onions, sliced
1/4 c. shredded Swiss cheese
1 t. pepper
5 eggs
3 egg whites
1 c. milk

Brown sausage in a skillet over medium-high heat; drain and transfer to a bowl. To the same skillet, add oil and mushrooms. Cook, stirring often, until golden, about 5 to 7 minutes. Add mushrooms to sausage. Stir in green onions, cheese and pepper. In a separate bowl, whisk together eggs, egg whites and milk. Divide egg mixture evenly among 12 lightly greased muffin cups. Sprinkle a heaping tablespoon of sausage mixture into each cup. Bake at 325 degrees for 25 minutes, or until tops are golden. Remove from cups; cool on a wire rack. Makes one dozen.

Rebecca Payerle
Dublin, OH

These mini quiches are so tasty and simple. Sometimes I whip them up and take them to work for my coworkers... they love them!

Corner Bakery

Maple-Pecan Brunch Ring

3/4 c. chopped pecans
1/2 c. brown sugar, packed
2 t. cinnamon
2 17.3-oz. tubes refrigerated
   jumbo flaky biscuits
2 T. butter, melted
1/2 c. maple syrup

Combine pecans, brown sugar and
cinnamon; set aside. Split each
biscuit horizontally; brush half of
the biscuits with butter and sprinkle
with half the pecan mixture. Arrange
topped biscuits in a circle on an
ungreased baking sheet; overlap each
biscuit slightly and keep within
2 inches of the edge of the baking
sheet. Brush remaining biscuit halves
with butter; sprinkle with remaining
pecan mixture. Arrange a second ring
just inside the first ring, overlapping
edges. Bake at 350 degrees for 30 to
35 minutes, until golden. Remove to
wire rack; cool 10 minutes. Brush
with maple syrup. Makes about
12 servings.

85

Leslie Williams
Americus, GA
A sweet & simple way to make
a tasty treat for guests.

Aunt Kornye's Cinnamon Rolls

3 envs. active dry yeast
2-1/2 c. warm water
4-1/2 c. all-purpose flour
18-1/2 oz. pkg. white cake mix
powdered sugar for dusting
1 c. butter, softened
1 c. brown sugar, packed
1/4 c. cinnamon
16-oz. container cream
   cheese icing

Dissolve yeast in very warm water, 110 to 115 degrees. Add flour and dry cake mix; stir and knead until smooth. Transfer to a greased bowl; cover with a tea towel and let rise until double in bulk, about 1-1/2 hours. Punch dough down, cover and let rise again until double in bulk, another hour. Roll out dough 1/2-inch thick on a surface dusted with powdered sugar; cut into 2 rectangles. Combine butter, brown sugar and cinnamon; spread equally over each rectangle. Roll up jelly-roll style, starting with a long end. Slice into 2-inch-thick slices. Place on a greased baking sheet and let rise for 30 minutes. Bake at 375 degrees for 20 minutes, or until golden. Cool slightly; spread with icing. Makes 10 to 15.

Ruby Kelsey
Holts Summit, MO

This recipe was found in my great-great-aunt Kornye's handwritten recipe book. At the bottom of the card she wrote "May increase waist size."

Apple Jack Muffins

2-1/3 c. all-purpose flour
1 c. plus 3 T. sugar, divided
1 T. baking powder
4 t. cinnamon, divided
1 t. baking soda
1/2 t. salt
1-1/2 c. apples, peeled, cored
   and finely chopped
1 c. buttermilk
1/3 c. milk
1/3 c. ricotta cheese
3 T. oil
1 T. vanilla extract
2 egg whites
1 egg, beaten

In a large bowl, sift together flour, one cup sugar, baking powder, 2 teaspoons cinnamon, baking soda and salt. Fold in apples; stir, then make a well in the center. Whisk together remaining ingredients; pour into well in flour mixture. Gently stir until just moistened. Spoon batter equally into 18 greased muffin cups. Combine remaining sugar and cinnamon; sprinkle evenly over batter. Bake at 400 degrees for 18 minutes, or until a toothpick inserted in a muffin tests clean. Makes 1-1/2 dozen.

Zoe Bennett
Columbia, SC

The best combination...
apples and cinnamon!

Blueberry Oatmeal Crisp

4 c. blueberries
1 c. all-purpose flour, divided
3/4 c. brown sugar, packed
3/4 c. long-cooking oats,
    uncooked
1/2 t. cinnamon
1/4 t. nutmeg
5 to 6 T. butter

Combine blueberries with 1/4 cup flour in a greased 11"x7" baking pan; mix thoroughly. In a bowl, combine remaining flour and other ingredients except butter. Cut in butter until coarse crumbs form; sprinkle over blueberries. Bake at 350 degrees for 25 minutes, or until top is golden and blueberries are bubbly. Makes 6 to 8 servings.

Amy Bastian
Mifflinburg, PA

This crisp is perfect on a brisk fall morning. Paired with some hot tea, it'll keep you warm and full all day!

Hot Chocolate Muffins

1/2 c. butter, softened
1 c. sugar
4 eggs, separated
6 T. hot chocolate mix
1/2 c. boiling water
2/3 c. milk
3 c. all-purpose flour
2 T. baking powder
1 t. salt
2 t. vanilla extract

Blend butter and sugar together in a large bowl; add egg yolks and beat until well mixed. In a separate bowl, dissolve hot chocolate mix in boiling water; add to butter mixture along with milk. Sift together flour, baking powder and salt; add to butter mixture. In a separate bowl, beat egg whites with an electric mixer on high speed until stiff peaks form; fold egg whites and vanilla into mixture. Pour into greased muffin tins until 3/4 full. Bake at 375 degrees for 20 to 25 minutes, until centers test done with a toothpick. Makes 1-1/2 to 2 dozen.

89

Carol Hickman
Kingsport, TN

A tasty breakfast treat for all the chocolate lovers out there!

Potato Doughnuts

2 envs. active dry yeast
1/2 c. warm water
1 c. sugar
3/4 c. shortening
1-1/2 c. mashed potatoes
3 eggs, beaten
2 c. milk
1 T. salt
1 T. lemon extract
6 to 8 c. all-purpose flour
oil for frying
Garnish: cinnamon-sugar,
  powdered sugar

Dissolve yeast in very warm water, 110 to 115 degrees; set aside. In a separate bowl, blend together sugar and shortening. Add potatoes, eggs, milk, salt, lemon extract and yeast mixture; mix well. Add in flour; mix and knead well until a soft dough forms. Place dough in a greased bowl; cover with a tea towel and let rise in a warm place until double in size, about one hour. Roll out dough 1/2-inch thick; cut with a doughnut cutter. Let doughnuts rise, uncovered, about 30 minutes. In a deep saucepan, heat several inches of oil to 375 degrees. Fry doughnuts, a few at a time, until golden; drain. Sprinkle with cinnamon-sugar or powdered sugar. Makes 4 dozen.

Emily Oravecz
New York, NY

What's better than a warm doughnut and a hot cup of coffee? These are also a great way to use up leftover mashed potatoes.

Cherry Turnovers

17-1/4 oz. pkg. frozen puff
    pastry, thawed
21-oz. can cherry pie filling,
    drained
1 c. powdered sugar
2 T. water

Separate puff pastry sheets and cut
each into 4 squares. Divide pie
filling evenly among squares. Brush
pastry edges with water and fold in
half diagonally. Seal and crimp edges
with a fork. With a knife, make a
small slit in tops of turnovers to
vent. Bake on an ungreased baking
sheet at 400 degrees for 15 to
18 minutes, until puffed and golden.
Let cool slightly. Blend together
powdered sugar and water; drizzle
over warm turnovers. Makes 8.

91

Lynda Robson
Boston, MA
These are so quick & easy
but taste like you spent
hours in the kitchen
making them!

Corner Bakery
Peanut Butter Crunch Coffee Cake

1 t. cinnamon
1-1/4 c. sugar, divided
1/2 c. butter, softened
1 c. sour cream
1 t. vanilla extract
2 eggs
2 c. all-purpose flour
1-1/2 t. baking powder
1 t. baking soda
1/4 t. salt
1/4 c. chopped pecans
4 chocolate-covered crispy
   peanut butter candy bars,
   crushed

Mix together cinnamon and 1/4 cup sugar; set aside. In a bowl, beat 1/2 cup butter until creamy. Beat in sour cream, vanilla and eggs. In a separate bowl, combine flour, baking powder, baking soda, remaining sugar and salt. Add to butter mixture; mix thoroughly. Spoon half the batter into a greased 8"x8" baking pan. Sprinkle with half each of the cinnamon-sugar, pecans and crushed candy bars. Pour remaining batter into pan; top with the remaining cinnamon-sugar, pecans and crushed candy bars. Bake at 325 degrees for 45 minutes. Cool in pan on a wire rack for 15 minutes. Makes 8 to 10 servings.

Pat Minnich
El Cajon, CA
This much-loved recipe has never been published before, but it did win an award at the county fair.

Cinnamon Cream Cheese Squares

2 8-oz. tubes refrigerated
   crescent rolls
8-oz. pkg. cream cheese,
   softened
1 t. vanilla extract
1/2 c. sugar
1/4 c. butter, melted
cinnamon-sugar to taste

Unroll one tube of crescent rolls
and arrange in a lightly greased
13"x9" baking pan; pinch seams
together. In a bowl, beat together
cream cheese, vanilla and sugar;
spread over rolls in pan. Top with
remaining tube of crescent rolls,
pinching together seams. Drizzle
melted butter over top layer of
crescents and sprinkle with
cinnamon-sugar. Bake at 350 degrees
for 30 minutes, or until golden.
Serves 10 to 12.

93

Jody Geary
Rockland, MA
I am asked to make these no
matter where I go! They're
scrumptious warm or cold.

Banana Chocolate-Toffee Drop Scones

2-1/2 c. biscuit baking mix
1/2 c. semi-sweet chocolate chips
1/2 c. toffee baking bits
1/4 c. plus 2 T. sugar, divided
1/4 c. whipping cream
1/2 t. vanilla extract
1 egg, beaten
3/4 c. ripe banana, mashed
1 T. milk

In a bowl, stir together baking mix, chocolate chips, toffee bits, 1/4 cup sugar, whipping cream, vanilla, egg and banana until a soft dough forms. Drop dough by 10 heaping tablespoonfuls onto greased baking sheets. Brush tops of scones with milk; sprinkle with remaining sugar. Bake at 425 degrees for 11 to 13 minutes, until golden. Makes 10.

Karen Puchnick
Butler, PA

There's something about the taste of banana and chocolate that just can't be beat... these scones capture that flavor perfectly.

Fresh Strawberry Bread

3 c. all-purpose flour
2 c. sugar
1-1/2 t. cinnamon
1 t. baking soda
1 t. salt
1 c. oil
4 eggs, beaten
2 c. strawberries, hulled and
   diced
Optional: 1-1/4 c. chopped nuts

In a bowl, combine flour, sugar,
cinnamon, baking soda and salt.
In a separate bowl, blend together
oil and eggs; fold in strawberries.
Gradually add egg mixture into flour
mixture; stir until just moistened.
Add nuts, if using. Pour into 2
greased and floured 9"x5" loaf pans.
Bake at 350 degrees for one hour.
Makes 2 loaves.

95

Mary Patenaude
Griswold, CT

A slice of this bread is
delicious served with
a dab of cream cheese or
homemade strawberry jam.

Ginger & Currant Scones

1 egg, beaten
3 T. brown sugar, packed
1 t. rum or rum-flavored extract
1 t. baking powder
2 T. milk
1 c. all-purpose flour
1/4 c. butter, softened
3/4 c. currants
2 T. candied ginger, chopped

In a large bowl, mix together all ingredients until well blended. Divide dough into 8 to 10 balls; flatten. Arrange scones on ungreased baking sheets. Bake at 350 degrees for 15 minutes, or until golden. Makes 8 to 10.

Selma Cherkas
Worcester, MA

The candied ginger adds a spicy sweetness to these scones that goes so well with the currants.

Corner Bakery

Monkey Bread

1/2 c. sugar
1-1/2 t. cinnamon
3 12-oz. tubes refrigerated
   biscuits, quartered
1 c. brown sugar, packed
1/2 c. butter, melted
2 T. water

Combine sugar and cinnamon in a bowl. Roll biscuit pieces in sugar mixture; place in a greased Bundt® pan. Combine brown sugar, butter and water; pour over biscuits. Bake at 350 degrees for 30 minutes. Invert onto a serving plate. Serves 6 to 8.

97

Michelle Pettit
Sebree, KY

This scrumptious dish is always a big hit. I usually have to make two batches because someone will always try to sneak away with one to take home!

Raised Doughnuts

2 c. boiling water
1/2 c. sugar
1 T. salt
2 T. shortening
2 envs. active dry yeast
2 eggs, beaten
7 c. all-purpose flour
oil for frying
Garnish: additional sugar for
    coating

Stir water, sugar, salt and shortening together in a large bowl; sprinkle yeast on top. Set aside; cool to room temperature. Blend in eggs; gradually add flour. Cover and let rise until double in bulk. Roll out dough 1/2-inch thick; cut with a doughnut cutter. Cover doughnuts and let rise until double in bulk, about 1-1/2 hours. In a deep saucepan, heat several inches of oil to 360 degrees. Fry doughnuts, a few at a time, until golden; drain. Spoon sugar into a paper bag; add doughnuts and shake to coat. Makes about 4 dozen.

Pam James
Delaware, OH

Every Tuesday night while I was growing up, my grandmother would make this dough for homemade doughnuts...even now, nothing compares to them.

Overnight Caramel Pecan Rolls

2 3.4-oz. pkgs. instant
    butterscotch pudding mix
1 c. brown sugar, packed
1 c. chopped pecans
1/2 c. chilled butter
36 frozen rolls, divided

Combine dry pudding mixes, brown sugar and pecans in a bowl. Cut in butter; set aside. Arrange half the frozen rolls in a lightly greased Bundt® pan. Sprinkle half the pudding mixture over top. Repeat layering with remaining rolls and pudding mixture. Cover loosely; refrigerate overnight. Bake at 350 degrees for one hour. Invert onto a serving plate. Serves 10 to 12.

99

Laura Carter
Vinita, OK

I got this recipe from my grandmother and mother... it's a family favorite that we all enjoy.

Corner Bakery

Cranberry-Orange Scones

2 c. all-purpose flour
10 t. sugar, divided
1 T. orange zest
1/4 t. baking soda
2 t. baking powder
1/2 t. salt
1/3 c. chilled butter, sliced
1 c. sweetened dried cranberries
1/4 c. plus 1 T. orange juice,
   divided
1/4 c. half-and-half
1 egg, beaten
1 T. milk
1/2 c. powdered sugar

Combine flour, 7 teaspoons sugar, orange zest, baking soda, baking powder and salt; cut in butter until coarse crumbs form. In a small bowl, stir together cranberries, 1/4 cup orange juice, half-and-half and egg. Add to flour mixture and mix until a soft dough forms. Knead 6 to 8 times on a lightly floured surface; pat into an 8-inch circle. Cut into 8 wedges; separate wedges and place on an ungreased baking sheet. Brush with milk; sprinkle with remaining sugar. Bake at 400 degrees for 12 to 15 minutes; cool slightly. Combine powdered sugar and remaining orange juice; drizzle over warm scones. Makes 8.

Dayna Hansen
Junction City, OR

My sisters and I always gather for an annual "sisters brunch." We each share special moments, gifts and yummy dishes. These scones are a favorite!

Sweet Twists

1 env. active dry yeast
1/4 c. warm water
3-3/4 c. all-purpose flour
1-1/2 t. salt
1 c. butter
2 eggs, beaten
1/2 c. sour cream
3 t. vanilla extract, divided
1-1/2 c. sugar

Dissolve yeast in very warm water, 110 to 115 degrees; set aside. Mix flour and salt in a large bowl; cut in butter until coarse crumbs form. Blend in eggs, sour cream, one teaspoon vanilla and yeast mixture; cover and chill overnight. Combine sugar and remaining vanilla. Sprinkle 1/2 cup vanilla-sugar mixture on a flat surface; roll out dough into a 16-inch by 8-inch rectangle. Sprinkle one tablespoon of vanilla-sugar mixture over dough; fold dough over and roll into a rectangle again. Continue sprinkling mixture, folding and rolling until no vanilla-sugar remains. Cut dough into 4-inch by 1-inch strips; twist strips and place on greased baking sheets. Bake at 350 degrees for 15 to 20 minutes. Makes 2 dozen.

IOI

Mary Jane Tolman
Rocky Mount, NC

These go great with
a tall glass of cold
milk for dunking.

Sweet Berry Popover

1 c. milk
1 T. butter, melted
1/2 t. vanilla extract
1/4 c. plus 1 T. sugar, divided
1/4 t. salt
1/8 t. nutmeg
1 c. all-purpose flour
2 eggs, beaten
1 c. berries
1/4 t. cinnamon

In a large bowl, whisk together milk, butter, vanilla, 1/4 cup sugar, salt and nutmeg; blend in flour. Gradually mix in eggs; set aside. Butter a 9" pie plate; add berries in a single layer into center of plate. Gently pour batter on top. Combine remaining sugar with cinnamon; sprinkle over batter. Bake at 450 degrees for 20 minutes. Lower heat to 350 degrees; continue baking until popover is golden, about 20 additional minutes. Slice into wedges; serve immediately. Makes 8 servings.

Elisabeth Macmillan
Burnaby, British Columbia
Use the freshest berries of the season for a deliciously different breakfast.

Morning Glory Muffins

2 c. all-purpose flour
1-1/4 c. sugar
2 t. baking soda
2 t. cinnamon
1/2 t. salt
2 c. carrots, peeled and grated
1/2 c. raisins
1/2 c. chopped pecans
3 eggs, beaten
1 c. oil
1 apple peeled, cored and
    shredded
2 t. vanilla extract

103

In a large bowl, combine flour, sugar, baking soda, cinnamon and salt. Stir in carrots, raisins and pecans. In a separate bowl, combine eggs, oil, apple and vanilla. Add egg mixture to flour mixture; stir until just combined. Spoon into greased or paper-lined muffin cups, filling 3/4 full. Bake at 350 degrees for 15 to 18 minutes, until golden. Makes 1-1/2 dozen.

Violet Leonard
Chesapeake, VA

These muffins are fantastic and filling. You can keep them in the freezer and thaw as needed.

Corner Bakery

Homemade Bagels

1 env. active dry yeast
1 c. warm water
2 T. sugar
1-1/2 t. salt
2-3/4 c. all-purpose flour,
    divided
Garnish: favorite-flavor cream
    cheese

In a large bowl, dissolve yeast in very warm water, 110 to 115 degrees. Add sugar, salt and half the flour to the yeast mixture; mix until smooth. Stir in remaining flour. Knead dough for 10 minutes on a lightly floured surface. Cover and let rise in a warm place until double in bulk. Punch down and divide into 8 equal pieces. Form each piece into a doughnut shape; let rise for 20 minutes. Bring a large pot of water to a boil; add bagels and boil for 7 minutes, turning once. Remove from water and place on a greased baking sheet. Bake at 375 degrees for 30 to 35 minutes, until golden. Cool slightly; slice and top with cream cheese. Makes 8 bagels.

Phyllis Peters
Three Rivers, MI

My daughter-in-law shared
this recipe...the bagels are
simple to make and so good.

Corner Bakery

Spiced Zucchini Bars

2 c. all-purpose flour
2 t. baking soda
1/2 t. salt
2 t. cinnamon
3 eggs, beaten
1 c. oil
2 c. sugar
1 t. vanilla extract
1 t. lemon juice
1 c. raisins
2 c. zucchini, grated
3/4 c. chopped nuts
16-oz. container cream cheese
   icing

In a bowl, combine flour, baking
soda, salt and cinnamon; set aside.
In a separate bowl, whisk together
eggs, oil, sugar, vanilla and lemon
juice. Gradually add flour mixture
to egg mixture. Fold in remaining
ingredients except frosting; pour
into a greased and floured
15"x10" jelly-roll pan. Bake at
325 degrees for 25 to 35 minutes,
until lightly golden. Cool; spread
with icing. Cut into bars.
Makes 3 dozen.

Erin Carnes
Gaines, MI

These yummy bars are one of
the first treats I make when
the zucchini is ready to
pick in my garden.

Lemon Coffee Cake

1 c. chopped walnuts
1/2 c. sugar
2 t. cinnamon
18-1/4 oz. pkg. yellow cake mix
  with pudding
3.4-oz. pkg. instant lemon
  pudding mix
8-oz. container sour cream
4 eggs, lightly beaten
1/2 c. oil

In a small bowl, combine walnuts, sugar and cinnamon; set aside. In a separate bowl, combine dry cake mix, dry pudding mix, sour cream, eggs and oil. Beat with an electric mixer on medium speed for 2 minutes. Pour into a greased 13"x9" baking pan. Sprinkle half of walnut mixture over batter. Spoon remaining batter evenly over top. Sprinkle with remaining walnut mixture. Bake at 350 degrees for 30 to 35 minutes, until cake tests done. Makes 12 to 16 servings.

Patty Fosnight
Wildorado, TX
I always take this tasty coffee cake to brunches. Everyone loves it and asks me for the recipe.

Pumpkin Streusel Coffee Cake

18-1/2 oz. pkg. yellow cake mix
1 c. canned pumpkin
3 eggs, beaten
3 T. oil
1/3 c. water
1 t. pumpkin pie spice
1-1/3 c. brown sugar, packed
  and divided
2 t. cinnamon, divided
1 c. all-purpose flour
1/2 c. butter, softened

In a bowl, combine dry cake mix, pumpkin, eggs, oil, water and pie spice. Pour half the batter into a greased 13"x9" baking pan; set aside remaining batter. Mix together 1/3 cup brown sugar and 3/4 teaspoon cinnamon; sprinkle over batter in pan. Carefully spread remaining batter over cinnamon mixture. Combine flour with remaining brown sugar, remaining cinnamon and butter; mix well. Spread evenly over top. Bake at 325 degrees for 30 to 40 minutes, until a knife tip inserted in the center tests clean. Serves 10 to 12.

107

Victoria Mitchel
Gettysburg, PA
I adapted my favorite coffee cake recipe to come up with this pumpkin version. It tastes so good with a cup of coffee on a cool fall day.

Corner Bakery

Whole-Grain Jam Squares

2 c. quick-cooking oats,
  uncooked
1-3/4 c. all-purpose flour
3/4 t. salt
1/2 t. baking soda
1 c. butter, softened
1 c. brown sugar, packed
1/2 c. chopped walnuts
1 t. cinnamon
3/4 to 1 c. strawberry preserves

Combine all ingredients except
preserves in a bowl; stir until large
crumbs form. Reserve 2 cups oat
mixture and set aside. Press
remaining mixture into a greased
13"x9" baking pan. Spread preserves
over the top; sprinkle with reserved
oat mixture. Bake at 400 degrees for
25 to 30 minutes, until golden. Cool;
cut into squares. Makes 2 dozen.

Ellen Gibson
Orlando, FL
These look so tempting
stacked on a jadite serving
plate, and their taste is
out of this world.

Yummy Yogurt Muffins

1-1/2 c. all-purpose flour
1 c. sugar
2 t. salt
8-oz. container favorite-flavor
  yogurt
1/2 c. oil
2 eggs, beaten
Optional: cinnamon-sugar

In a bowl, combine all ingredients
except cinnamon-sugar, mixing well.
Fill 12 paper-lined muffin cups
2/3 full with batter. Top each cup
with cinnamon-sugar, if using. Bake
at 350 degrees for 25 to 30 minutes,
until golden. Makes one dozen.

Trisha Donley
Pinedale, WY

These muffins are so fast
and easy to make. With so
many varieties of yogurt,
you could have a different
flavor every time!

Spicy Cabbage–Apple Slaw, page 155

Refrigerator Pickles, page 208

Chicken Corn Chowder, page 131

Texas Steak Sandwich, page 188

101 Soups, Salads & Sandwiches

German Green Beans, page 156

Green Pepper Soup, page 115

Grilled Chicken & Zucchini Wraps, page 180

Oodles of our tried & true soup, salad and sandwich recipes are perfect to mix and match...there's an endless variety of delectable, lip-smacking lunches.

Mustard & Thyme Potato Salad, page 151

Scott's Ham & Pear Sandwiches, page 175

Chicken Enchilada Soup, page 133

Tips for Quick & Tasty Soups, Salads & Sandwiches

★ Making a favorite soup for supper? Let the slow cooker help out! In the morning, toss in all the ingredients and turn it to the low setting. A recipe that simmers for one to two hours on the stovetop can usually cook all day on low without overcooking.

★ Grilled cheese and tomato soup…is there anything more comforting? For delicious soup in a jiffy, heat together a can of condensed tomato soup and a can of diced tomatoes until hot. Stir in a little cream.

★ Give salads a fresh new taste…instead of using white vinegar when making salad dressing, add a splash of fruit juice or fruit-flavored vinegar.

★ Serving fruit salad? Just for fun, spoon it into a hollowed-out watermelon, honeydew or cantaloupe, or slide fruit slices onto wooden skewers.

★ Whip up a hearty panini sandwich or two. No fancy panini grill is needed…a countertop grill will do! Layer bread with deli meat and cheese slices, spread a little softened butter on the outside and grill until toasty.

Spicy Sausage Chowder

16-oz. pkg. sweet Italian pork
   sausage links, diced
1 onion, finely chopped
2 cloves garlic, minced
15-oz. can diced tomatoes
4-oz. can chopped green chiles
15-1/4 oz. can corn
14-1/2 oz. can chicken broth
8-oz. jar enchilada sauce
1 t. dried oregano
1 t. chili powder
1 t. salt
1 t. pepper
2 c. water

In a skillet over medium heat, cook
sausage until golden; drain. In a
slow cooker, stir in sausage and
remaining ingredients. Cover and
cook on low setting for 6 to 8 hours,
or on high setting for 3 to 4 hours.
Serve with Tortilla Crisps. Serves 4
to 6.

Tortilla Crisps:

4 whole-wheat tortillas
olive oil

Lightly brush both sides of tortillas
with olive oil. Cut into wedges. Bake
at 400 degrees on an ungreased
baking sheet for 8 to 10 minutes,
until crisp.

113

Sarah Gardner
Clifton Park, NY

This easy recipe has become
a staple in our household
during the holidays. Just
add all ingredients to the
slow cooker and leave it
to work its magic!

Chicken Noodle Gumbo

2 lbs. boneless, skinless chicken
    breasts, cut into 1-inch cubes
4 16-oz. cans chicken broth
15-oz. can diced tomatoes
32-oz. pkg. frozen okra, corn,
    celery and red pepper mixed
    vegetables
8-oz. pkg. bowtie pasta, uncooked
1/2 t. garlic powder
salt and pepper to taste

Place chicken, broth and tomatoes in
a large soup pot. Bring to a boil over
medium heat. Reduce heat; simmer
10 minutes. Add frozen vegetables,
uncooked pasta and seasonings. Return
to a boil. Cover and simmer one hour.
Serves 8 to 10.

Lorrie Smith
Drummonds, TN

This colorful dish makes
enough to feed a whole bunch
of hungry folks! Look for the
"gumbo blend" of frozen
vegetables at the market.

Green Pepper Soup

2 lbs. ground beef
28-oz. can tomato sauce
28-oz. can diced tomatoes
2 c. cooked rice
2 c. green peppers, chopped
2 cubes beef bouillon
1/4 c. brown sugar, packed
2 t. pepper

In a stockpot over medium heat, brown beef; drain. Add remaining ingredients and bring to a boil. Reduce heat; cover and simmer for 30 to 40 minutes, until peppers are tender. Makes 8 to 10 servings.

115

Sharon Laney
Mogadore, OH

Fall brings thoughts of a bountiful harvest with gardens and roadside stands overflowing with fresh vegetables...and this hearty soup.

Kielbasa Soup

1 head cabbage, shredded
16-oz. pkg. Kielbasa sausage, sliced
2 16-oz. cans diced tomatoes
1 onion, chopped
2 zucchini, quartered and sliced
2 yellow squash, quartered and
   sliced
2 T. seasoned salt
2 cloves garlic, crushed
1 cube beef bouillon
1 t. dried oregano
2 redskin or russet potatoes, cubed

In a stockpot, combine all ingredients
except potatoes. Cover ingredients with
water; bring to a boil. Cover, reduce
heat and simmer for 1-1/2 to 2 hours.
Add potatoes during last 30 minutes of
cook time. Makes 8 to 10 servings.

Pamela Bennett
Whittier, CA

My mom made up this recipe
one evening when there
wasn't a lot to eat in the
house. It has since become
a favorite comfort food!

Chicken & Dumplin' Soup

10-3/4 oz. can cream of chicken
soup
4 c. chicken broth
4 boneless, skinless chicken
breasts, cooked and shredded
2 15-oz. cans mixed vegetables
2 12-oz. tubes refrigerated
biscuits, quartered

Bring soup and broth to a slow boil
in a saucepan over medium heat;
whisk until smooth. Stir in chicken
and vegetables; bring to a boil. Drop
biscuit quarters into soup; cover and
simmer for 15 minutes. Remove
from heat. Let stand 10 minutes
before serving. Serves 4 to 6.

117

Brenda Hancock
Hartford, NY
This is truly comfort food at
its finest. And with the help
of refrigerated biscuits, it
couldn't be easier!

Surprise Bean Soup

16-oz. pkg. bacon, cut into
   1-inch pieces
1 onion, chopped
1 c. carrot, peeled and diced
1 c. celery, chopped
15-oz. can tomato sauce
15-oz. can diced tomatoes
1 c. chicken broth
2 15-oz. cans navy beans, drained
3/4 c. creamy peanut butter
1/2 t. pepper

In a skillet over medium heat, cook
bacon until crisp; drain. Return bacon
to skillet; stir in onion, carrot and
celery, cooking until onion is
translucent. In a large stockpot over
medium heat, stir together bacon
mixture, tomato sauce, diced tomatoes,
chicken broth and beans until hot and
bubbly. Stir in peanut butter and
pepper until well combined. Serve
immediately. Makes 6 servings.

Susan Jacobs
Vista, CA
My hubby took my bean soup
recipe and added his favorite
ingredient...peanut butter!

Meatball-Vegetable Cheese Soup

1 lb. ground beef
1/4 c. dry bread crumbs
1 egg, beaten
1/2 t. salt
1/2 t. hot pepper sauce
1 c. celery, chopped
1/2 c. onion, chopped
2 cubes beef bouillon
1 c. corn
1 c. potato, peeled and diced
1/2 c. carrot, peeled and sliced
2 c. water
16-oz. jar pasteurized process
    cheese sauce

119

In a bowl, mix together beef, bread crumbs, egg, salt and hot sauce; form into one-inch balls. Place in a slow cooker. Add remaining ingredients except cheese sauce. Cover and cook on low setting for 8 to 10 hours. Immediately before serving, stir in cheese sauce until combined. Cover and cook an additional 10 minutes, until warmed through. Serves 6.

Denise Webb
Galveston, IN

You'll want to try this slow-cooker recipe...it's a real family-pleaser!

Cream of Zucchini Soup

3 lbs. zucchini, sliced
   1/2-inch thick
2 onions, quartered
5 slices bacon
4 c. chicken broth
1 t. salt
1 t. pepper
Optional: 1/2 t. garlic powder
Garnish: onion and garlic
   croutons, or butter and grated
   Parmesan cheese

Combine all ingredients except garnish
in a soup pot over medium heat. Cook
until zucchini is tender and bacon is
cooked, about 45 minutes. Ladle soup
into a blender and process until
smooth. Return to soup pot; heat
through. Serve topped with croutons or
with a pat of butter and a sprinkling of
Parmesan cheese. Makes 6 servings.

Susan Maurer
Dahlgren, IL
One taste and you'll
agree...there's really
no such thing as too
many zucchini!

Chilled Melon Soup

3 c. cantaloupe melon, peeled,
    seeded and chopped
2 T. sugar, divided
1/4 c. orange juice, divided
1/8 t. salt, divided
3 c. honeydew melon, peeled,
    seeded and chopped
Garnish: fresh mint sprigs or
    orange slices

In a blender, process cantaloupe, half
the sugar, half the juice and half the
salt until smooth. Cover and
refrigerate. Repeat with honeydew
and remaining ingredients except
garnish. Refrigerate, covered, in
separate containers. To serve, pour
equal amounts of each mixture at the
same time on opposite sides of
individual soup bowls. Garnish as
desired. Makes 4 to 6 servings.

121

Janice Woods
Northern Cambria, PA
This tasty and beautiful
recipe is perfect for summer
get-togethers with friends.

Pepper Jack-Crab Bisque

2 T. butter
2 stalks celery, finely chopped
1 onion, finely chopped
2 10-3/4 oz. cans tomato bisque
   or tomato soup
2-1/2 c. whipping cream or
   half-and-half
3 8-oz. pkgs. imitation crabmeat,
   flaked
1-1/2 c. shredded Pepper Jack
   cheese

Melt butter in a stockpot over medium heat. Add celery and onion; cook until softened. Add bisque or soup, cream or half-and-half and crabmeat. Simmer over low heat until heated through; stir in cheese. If too thick, add a little more cream or half-and-half as desired. Makes 6 servings.

Wendy Ball
Battle Creek, MI
My husband and I had enjoyed a soup like this when dining out with our good friends, Rick and Carolyn. My efforts to recreate it really paid off...we love it!

Beef Stew & Biscuits

1 lb. ground beef
1/4 c. onion, chopped
1/4 t. dried basil
1/8 t. pepper
3-1/2 c. frozen or canned mixed
    vegetables
2 8-oz. cans tomato sauce
1 c. sharp Cheddar cheese, cubed
12-oz. tube refrigerated biscuits

In a skillet, brown beef and onion; drain. Add seasonings, mixed vegetables and tomato sauce; mix well. Cover and simmer for 5 minutes. Fold in cheese cubes; pour into an ungreased 2-quart casserole dish. Arrange biscuits on top. Bake, uncovered, at 375 degrees for 25 minutes, or until biscuits are golden. Serves 4 to 6.

123

Jocelyn Medina
Phoenixville, PA

This tried & true one-pot meal is perfect for Sunday dinner.

Creamy Chicken & Wild Rice Soup

4 boneless, skinless chicken
   breasts, cubed
3/4 lb. carrot, peeled and sliced
3 stalks celery, sliced
1 onion, diced
2 4.3-oz. pkgs. long-grain and
   wild rice mix
4 10-3/4 oz. cans cream of potato
   soup
32-oz. container chicken broth
2 c. whipping cream

In a slow cooker, layer chicken, carrot, celery, onion, rice with seasoning packets and potato soup. Pour broth over top. Cover and cook on low setting for 8 hours. Stir thoroughly. Mix in cream; cover and heat through, about 15 minutes. Serves 8 to 10.

Patty Habig Bowen
Westfield, NY

I've tweaked this slow-cooker recipe so many times, it's nothing like the original! It's so thick, you can use the leftovers for chicken pot pie filling.

Fred's Chunky Chili

1 lb. ground beef or turkey,
   browned and drained
3/4 c. green pepper, diced
1 t. garlic, minced
3/4 c. onion, diced
6-oz. can tomato paste
14-1/2 oz. can stewed tomatoes
15-1/2 oz. can kidney beans
1/4 c. salsa
1 T. sugar
1/2 t. cayenne pepper
1/2 t. dried cilantro
1 t. dried basil
Garnish: shredded Cheddar
   cheese, crackers

125

Combine all ingredients except
garnish in a Dutch oven. Bring to
a simmer over medium-high heat.
Cover and simmer over low heat for
30 minutes, stirring occasionally.
Serve with cheese and crackers.
Serves 4 to 6.

Marian Muder
Hubbard, OH

My husband has been
making his signature chili
for years now. It's a
combination of several
tasty recipes.

Pioneer Beef Stew

14-1/2 oz. can petite diced
   tomatoes
1 c. water
3 T. quick-cooking tapioca,
   uncooked
2 t. sugar
1-1/2 t. salt
1/2 t. pepper
1-1/2 lbs. stew beef, cubed
3 to 4 potatoes, peeled and cubed
4 carrots, peeled and thickly sliced
1 onion, diced

In a large bowl, combine tomatoes with
juice, water, tapioca, sugar, salt and
pepper. Mix well; stir in remaining
ingredients. Pour into a greased
3-quart casserole dish. Cover and bake
at 375 degrees for 1-1/2 to 2 hours,
until beef and vegetables are tender.
Serves 4 to 6.

Angie O'Keefe
Soddy Daisy, TN

There's nothing more
satisfying than a hearty
bowl of beef stew! It's
baked, not simmered on the
stovetop...no need to
watch it.

Macaroni & Cheese Chowder

14-oz. can chicken broth
1 c. water
1 c. elbow macaroni, uncooked
1 c. milk
8-oz. pkg. pasteurized process
    cheese spread
1 c. cooked ham, diced
1 c. corn

Over medium heat, bring broth and
water to a boil in a saucepan. Add
macaroni and cook until tender,
about 12 minutes. Reduce heat to
low. Add milk, cheese, ham and
corn. Simmer and stir until cheese
is melted. Serves 4 to 6.

127

Alissa Sellers
Bangor, PA

This recipe is a family
favorite that even my young
son loves! It's perfect for
a quick family dinner,
especially on a cold
or rainy night.

Chill-Chaser Pork Stew

2 to 2-1/2 lbs. pork steaks, cubed
2 T. olive oil
2 sweet onions, chopped
2 green peppers, chopped
2 cloves garlic, minced
salt and pepper to taste
6-oz. can tomato paste
28-oz. can diced tomatoes
2 8-oz. cans sliced mushrooms,
   drained

In a Dutch oven over medium heat,
sauté pork in oil until browned. Add
onions, green peppers, garlic, salt and
pepper. Cover; cook over medium heat
until pork is tender. Add tomato paste,
tomatoes with juice and mushrooms;
bring to a boil. Reduce heat to low;
simmer for one hour, stirring often.
Serves 6.

Kathy McCann-Neff
Claxton, GA

After a day of raking
leaves, this stew warms
and rejuvenates you!

Creamy Split Pea Soup

1 lb. bacon, crisply cooked,
   crumbled and 2 to 3 T.
   drippings reserved
1 onion, diced
2 stalks celery, diced
8 c. water
16-oz. pkg. dried split peas
2 potatoes, peeled and diced
2 t. salt
1/4 t. pepper
3 cubes beef bouillon
1 bay leaf
1 c. half-and-half

129

Heat reserved bacon drippings in a
large soup pot; sauté onion and
celery over medium heat until tender.
Add remaining ingredients except
half-and-half; bring to a boil over
medium-high heat. Reduce heat
to low; cover and simmer for
45 minutes, until peas are very
tender. Discard bay leaf. Fill a
blender 3/4 full with soup; blend
to purée. Return to soup pot; stir
in half-and-half. Simmer over
medium heat for 5 minutes, until
heated through. Garnish with
reserved bacon. Serves 8.

Kathy Schroeder
Vermilion, OH

This soup was a sensation
at my daughter's baby
shower...so much flavor!

Tomato-Ravioli Soup

1 lb. ground beef
28-oz. can crushed tomatoes
6-oz. can tomato paste
2 c. water
1-1/2 c. onion, chopped
2 cloves garlic, minced
1/4 c. fresh parsley, chopped
3/4 t. dried basil
1/2 t. dried oregano
1/4 t. dried thyme
1/2 t. onion salt
1/2 t. salt
1/4 t. pepper
1/2 t. sugar
9-oz. pkg. frozen cheese ravioli
1/4 c. grated Parmesan cheese

In a Dutch oven, cook beef over medium heat until no longer pink; drain. Stir in tomatoes with juice, tomato paste, water, onion, garlic, seasonings and sugar. Bring to a boil. Reduce heat; cover and simmer for 30 minutes. Meanwhile, cook ravioli as package directs; drain. Add ravioli to soup and heat through. Stir in Parmesan cheese; serve immediately. Makes 6 to 8 servings.

Heather Quinn
Gilmer, TX

This soup has a light, smooth flavor...there's always an empty pot afterwards!

Chicken Corn Chowder

1-1/2 c. milk
10-1/2 oz. can chicken broth
10-3/4 oz. can cream of chicken
   soup
10-3/4 oz. can cream of potato
   soup
1 to 2 10-oz. cans chicken,
   drained
1/3 c. green onion, chopped
11-oz. can sweet corn & diced
   peppers
4-oz. can chopped green chiles,
   drained
8-oz. pkg. shredded Cheddar
   cheese

131

Mix together all ingredients except
cheese in a stockpot. Cook over
low heat, stirring frequently, for
15 minutes, or until heated through.
Add cheese; stir until melted. Serves
6 to 8.

Katie French
Portland, TX

A quick main dish that goes
great with a big, buttery
piece of cornbread.

Swiss Potato Soup

12 slices bacon, coarsely chopped
1 onion, chopped
4 green onions, coarsely chopped
6 c. cabbage, coarsely chopped
4 potatoes, peeled and diced
6 c. chicken broth
2 c. Gruyère cheese, shredded
1 c. light cream
1 T. dill weed
salt and pepper to taste

Sauté bacon in a large stockpot for
3 minutes. Drain, reserving
2 tablespoons drippings in skillet.
Add onions and cabbage; cook
5 minutes. Add potatoes and broth;
bring to a boil. Reduce heat and
simmer 40 minutes. Pour into a
blender, a little at a time, and blend
until smooth. Pour back into stockpot.
Add cheese gradually, stirring to melt.
Do not boil. Stir in remaining
ingredients just before serving.
Serves 6 to 8.

Vickie
Sometimes I'll replace the
green onions with two
leeks...scrumptious
either way!

Chicken Enchilada Soup

1 onion, chopped
1 clove garlic, pressed
1 to 2 t. oil
14-1/2 oz. can beef broth
14-1/2 oz. can chicken broth
10-3/4 oz. can cream of chicken
   soup
1-1/2 c. water
12-1/2 oz. can chicken, drained
4-oz. can chopped green chiles
2 t. Worcestershire sauce
1 T. steak sauce
1 t. ground cumin
1 t. chili powder
1/8 t. pepper
6 corn tortillas, cut into strips
1 c. shredded Cheddar cheese

In a stockpot over medium heat, sauté onion and garlic in oil. Add remaining ingredients except tortilla strips and cheese; bring to a boil. Cover; reduce heat and simmer for one hour, stirring occasionally. Uncover; stir in tortilla strips and cheese. Simmer an additional 10 minutes. Serves 6.

Jeanne Dinnel
Canby, OR

This recipe may look lengthy, but it goes together in a jiffy! Serve it with a simple salad of ripe tomato and avocado drizzled with lime vinaigrette dressing.

133

Chili Stew

1/2 onion, chopped
1/2 red pepper, chopped
1/2 yellow pepper, chopped
1 butternut squash, peeled
   and cubed
2 T. oil
1 T. garlic, chopped
1 lb. ground beef
1 T. smoked paprika
2 t. ground cumin
2 t. dried basil
2 t. dried thyme
1/8 to 1/4 t. Worcestershire sauce
28-oz. can plum tomatoes
28-oz. can diced tomatoes
15-1/2 oz. can kidney beans,
   drained and rinsed
15-1/2 oz. can black beans,
   drained and rinsed
2 T. all-purpose flour
2 c. beef broth
salt and pepper to taste

In a stockpot, cook onion, peppers and squash in oil until tender. Add garlic and beef. Cook until beef is browned; drain. Add spices, Worcestershire sauce, tomatoes and beans; break up tomatoes with a spoon. In a bowl, mix flour and broth; stir into chili. Bring to a boil. Reduce heat, cover and simmer for 30 minutes to 2 hours. Season with salt and pepper. Serves 6.

Linda Marshall
Gowganda, Ontario
I planned to make chili, only to discover that I had no chili powder. So I put this together instead, and now it's our favorite.

Clam & Scallop Chowder

2 onions, finely chopped
1/4 c. butter, divided
1 t. salt
1 t. pepper
1 c. chicken broth or water
2 potatoes, peeled and cubed
1/4 lb. bay scallops
10-oz. can baby clams, drained
    and 1/2 c. liquid reserved
1 c. light cream
1 c. milk
2 slices bacon, crisply cooked
    and crumbled

135

In a large heavy saucepan over medium heat, cook onions in 2 tablespoons butter for 5 minutes, or until tender. Add salt, pepper, broth or water and potatoes; cook until fork tender. Reduce heat; add scallops and cook just until tender, 4 to 5 minutes. Stir in clams with reserved liquid, cream, milk, bacon and remaining butter. Heat through without boiling for 3 minutes, or until hot. Serves 4.

Lisa Purcell
Kitchener, Ontario

For a special presentation, serve this steaming chowder in hollowed-out rounds of sourdough bread...oh-so good!

Kitchen Cabinet Mild White Chili

2 15-1/2 oz. cans great Northern beans
Optional: 4-1/2 oz. can diced green chiles
14-oz. can chicken broth
1 T. dried, minced onion
1 T. red pepper flakes
1-1/2 t. dried, minced garlic
1 t. ground cumin
1/2 t. dried oregano
1/8 t. cayenne pepper
1/8 t. ground cloves
1-1/2 c. cooked chicken, chopped
4-oz. can sliced mushrooms, drained
1 c. shredded sharp Cheddar cheese

In a Dutch oven, combine all ingredients except chicken, mushrooms and cheese. Cook over medium heat for 5 minutes; bring to a boil. Reduce heat and simmer 5 minutes. Add chicken and mushrooms; simmer, uncovered, for 8 to 10 minutes, until heated through. Serve with cheese. Makes 4 servings.

Becky Hall
Belton, MO

This recipe was created on a cold night with ingredients from the kitchen cabinet. It can easily be spiced up with a can of diced chiles or chopped jalapeño peppers.

BBQ Sloppy Joe Soup

1 lb. ground beef chuck
16-oz. can barbecue Sloppy Joe
    sauce
10-3/4 oz. can cream of potato
    soup
10-3/4 oz. can minestrone soup
1-1/4 c. water
15-oz. can light red kidney
    beans, drained and rinsed
14-1/2 oz. can green beans,
    drained
15-1/4 oz. can green peas,
    drained
15-oz. can diced tomatoes,
    drained
garlic powder and steak
    seasoning to taste
Garnish: oyster crackers

137

In a large saucepan over medium
heat, brown beef; drain. Stir in
Sloppy Joe sauce; heat through.
Add remaining ingredients except
crackers; simmer until bubbly, about
10 to 15 minutes. Serve with crackers.
Makes 6 to 8 servings.

Betty Lou Wright
Hendersonville, TN

This recipe was a happy
accident! One day I made
vegetable soup. Remembering
leftover Sloppy Joe sauce
in the fridge, I stirred it
into the soup. What a hit!

Bean & Sausage Soup

5 Italian pork sausage links
1/4 c. onion, diced
3 cloves garlic, minced
1 t. olive oil
1 t. salt
1/4 to 1/2 t. red pepper flakes
15-oz. can diced tomatoes
32-oz. container chicken broth
2 15-oz. cans white kidney beans
4 c. spinach, torn
Garnish: grated Parmesan cheese

In a Dutch oven, sauté sausage, onion
and garlic in oil until sausage is golden.
Remove sausage links and slice into
one-inch pieces; return to pot. Add
remaining ingredients except garnish.
Cover and bring to a boil. Reduce heat
to low; simmer, covered, for 2 to
3 hours. Garnish with cheese.
Serves 6.

Janet Parsons
Pickerington, OH
If you like pasta, cook
ditalini or elbows
separately and add
1/2 cup to each serving.

Grandma's Chicken Noodle Soup

16-oz. pkg. thin egg noodles,
   uncooked
1 t. oil
12 c. chicken broth
1-1/2 t. salt
1 t. poultry seasoning
1 c. celery, chopped
1 c. onion, chopped
Optional: 1 c. carrot, peeled
   and chopped
1/3 c. cornstarch
1/4 c. cold water
4 c. cooked chicken, diced

139

Bring a large pot of water to boil over medium-high heat; add noodles and oil. Cook according to package directions; drain and set aside. Combine broth, salt and poultry seasoning in the same pot; bring to a boil over medium heat. Stir in vegetables; reduce heat, cover and simmer for 15 minutes. Combine cornstarch with cold water in a small bowl; gradually add to soup, stirring constantly. Stir in chicken and noodles; heat through, about 5 to 10 minutes. Serves 8.

Evelyn Belcher
Monroeton, PA

My daughter gave me this
recipe years ago...now it's
my favorite!

Hungarian Mushroom Soup

1/4 c. onion, diced
8 c. sliced mushrooms
1 c. butter
1 c. all-purpose flour
2 16-oz. cans chicken broth
3 T. paprika
1/4 c. soy sauce
16-oz. container sour cream
1 T. dried parsley
1 T. dill weed
2 T. lemon juice
12-oz. can evaporated milk

In a stockpot over medium heat, sauté onion and mushrooms in butter, until tender. Stir in flour. Add remaining ingredients except evaporated milk; bring to a simmer. Stir in evaporated milk. Cover and simmer about one hour. Makes 8 to 10 servings.

Carleen Pettit
Sidney, OH

My family loves this creamy dish. It's so different from the typical soup.

Spicy Vegetable Soup

2 T. olive oil
2 onions, sliced
2 cloves garlic, minced
6 c. vegetable broth
1 c. celery, chopped
1 c. cauliflower flowerets
1 c. broccoli flowerets
1-1/2 c. green beans, sliced
4-oz. can diced green chiles
2 T. chili powder
1 T. dried oregano
1 T. ground cumin
1 t. paprika
1 t. ground sage

141

Heat oil in a large skillet over medium-high heat. Add onions and garlic; sauté until onions are tender, about 5 minutes. Transfer to a slow cooker. Add remaining ingredients, stirring to combine. Cover and cook on low setting for 6 to 7 hours. Makes 8 servings.

Sonya Labbe
Los Angeles, CA

When my vegetarian friend from New Mexico comes to visit, I'll make this slow-cooker recipe so I can spend more time with her!

Mom's Creamy Chicken Chowder

4 to 6 boneless, skinless chicken
  breasts, cubed
3 c. potatoes, peeled and cubed
12 c. chicken broth
3 cubes chicken bouillon
1 c. celery, diced
1/2 c. onion, diced
1-1/2 c. carrot, peeled and grated
1/2 c. butter
12-oz. can evaporated milk
1/2 c. water
1-1/2 c. all-purpose flour

Combine chicken, potatoes, broth,
bouillon, celery, onion and carrot in
a large pot. Simmer over medium heat
until chicken is cooked and vegetables
are tender. Stir in butter until melted;
set aside. In a blender, mix milk, water
and flour until smooth; add to soup
mixture. Cook and stir until thickened.
Serves 12 to 15.

Stephanie Swensen
Mapleton, UT

Paired with homemade bread or
rolls, this is my family's
most-requested soup.

Chicken Cacciatore Soup

1 c. rotini pasta, uncooked
3 14-1/2 oz. cans vegetable
   broth, divided
1/2 lb. boneless, skinless chicken
   breasts, cut into bite-size
   pieces
30-oz. jar extra-chunky spaghetti
   sauce with mushrooms
14-1/2 oz. can stewed tomatoes,
   chopped
1 zucchini, sliced
1 onion, chopped
2 cloves garlic, chopped
1/2 t. Italian seasoning
Optional: 1 T. red wine

Cook rotini according to package
directions, substituting one can
broth for part of the water; drain
and set aside. Combine remaining
ingredients in a large saucepan.
Simmer 20 to 30 minutes, until
chicken is cooked through and
vegetables are tender. Stir in rotini;
heat through. Serves 6 to 8.

143

Kathy Unruh
Fresno, CA
Go ahead and add a couple
drops of hot pepper sauce
for those who like it spicy!

Spring Ramen Salad

3-oz. pkg. chicken-flavored
    ramen noodles
1 t. sesame oil
1/2 c. seedless grapes, halved
1/2 c. apple, cored and diced
1/4 c. pineapple, diced
2 green onions, diced
1 c. cooked chicken, cubed
1 c. Muenster cheese, cubed
1-1/2 T. lemon juice
1/8 c. canola oil
1 t. sugar
Garnish: sesame seed

Set aside seasoning packet from ramen
noodles. Cook noodles according to
package directions. Drain noodles;
rinse with cold water. In a bowl, toss
sesame oil with noodles to coat. Stir
in fruit, onions, chicken and cheese.
In a separate bowl, whisk together
lemon juice, canola oil, sugar and
1/2 teaspoon of contents of seasoning
packet. Pour over noodle mixture; toss
to coat. Garnish with sesame seed.
Cover and chill before serving. Makes
4 servings.

Lori Rosenberg
University Heights, OH
This yummy recipe is truly
made to clean out the
fridge...you can put
almost anything in it!

Asian Summer Salad

8-oz. pkg. thin spaghetti,
uncooked and broken
into fourths
3/4 c. carrot, peeled and cut into
2-inch strips
3/4 c. zucchini, cut into
2-inch strips
3/4 c. red pepper, chopped
1/3 c. green onion, sliced
3/4 lb. deli roast turkey, cut
into 2-inch-long strips
Garnish: chopped peanuts,
chopped fresh cilantro

Cook pasta according to package
directions; drain and rinse with
cold water. In a bowl, combine all
ingredients except garnish. Toss with
Ginger Dressing. Refrigerate one
hour; garnish as desired. Makes
6 to 8 servings.

Ginger Dressing:

1/4 c. canola oil
3 T. rice vinegar
3 T. reduced-sodium soy sauce
2 t. sugar
1/8 t. fresh ginger, grated
1/8 t. cayenne pepper
1 clove garlic, chopped

Whisk together all ingredients.

145

**Rhonda Schmidt
Emporia, KS**

This salad is great in
the summertime when you
have ripe zucchini from
your garden. It is cool
and refreshing!

Panzanella Salad

1/2 loaf Italian or French bread, cubed
1/4 c. olive oil
salt and pepper to taste
1 red pepper, chopped
1 yellow pepper, chopped
1 orange pepper, chopped
1 cucumber, chopped
1 red onion, chopped
1 pt. cherry or grape tomatoes
1 to 2 T. capers
6 leaves fresh basil, cut into long, thin strips
3/4 c. vinaigrette or Italian salad dressing

In a bowl, toss together bread, olive oil, salt and pepper. Spread on an ungreased baking sheet and bake at 350 degrees for 5 minutes, or until golden and crisp; let cool. In a bowl, combine remaining ingredients. Just before serving, add bread cubes and toss to coat. Makes 6 to 8 servings.

Denise Herr
Galloway, OH

I've made this several times. It's a beautiful summer presentation salad and so delicious. Garden veggies are best but absolutely not necessary!

Tarragon Steak Dinner Salad

6 c. Boston lettuce
2 pears, peeled, cored and sliced
1/2 red onion, thinly sliced
1/2 lb. grilled beef steak, thinly
    sliced
1/4 c. crumbled blue cheese
1/2 c. red wine vinaigrette salad
    dressing
1 T. fresh tarragon, minced
1/4 t. pepper

Arrange lettuce, pears and onion
on 4 serving plates. Top with sliced
steak and sprinkle with cheese.
Combine dressing, tarragon and
pepper in a small bowl; whisk well.
Drizzle dressing mixture over salad.
Serves 4.

147

Amanda Dixon
Dublin, OH

Delicious...a perfect
light summer meal.

Emily's Frozen Fruit Salad

16-oz. can apricot halves
20-oz. can crushed pineapple
10-oz. pkg. frozen strawberries,
    thawed
6-oz. can frozen orange juice
    concentrate, thawed
1/2 c. water
1/2 c. sugar
3 bananas, sliced

Combine undrained apricots and
pineapple. Mix in remaining
ingredients except bananas; set aside.
Arrange bananas in a 13"x9" baking
pan; pour fruit mixture over top.
Cover and freeze for at least 24 hours.
Before serving, let stand at room
temperature for about 15 minutes.
Cut into squares to serve. Makes 10 to
12 servings.

Emily Hauschild
Hutchinson, KS

The best frozen fruit salad
I've ever eaten! Years ago
when I was in 4-H, I won
a purple ribbon with
this recipe.

Spinach & Clementine Salad

2 lbs. clementines, peeled and
  sectioned
2 16-oz. pkgs. baby spinach
4 stalks celery, thinly sliced on
  the diagonal
1 c. red onion, thinly sliced
1/2 c. pine nuts or walnuts,
  toasted
1/4 c. dried cherries
2 T. red wine vinegar
1/4 c. olive oil
1 t. Dijon mustard
1 clove garlic, minced
1/8 t. sugar
salt and pepper to taste

In a large salad bowl, combine
clementines, spinach, celery, onion,
nuts and cherries. Toss to mix well.
Whisk together remaining ingredients
in a small bowl; drizzle over salad.
Serve immediately. Makes 8 servings.

149

Sharon Jones
Oklahoma City, OK
This fresh, crunchy salad
is a perfect way to use
a Christmas gift box
of clementines.

Skillet-Toasted Corn Salad

1/3 c. plus 1 T. olive oil, divided
1/3 c. lemon juice
1 T. Worcestershire sauce
3 to 4 dashes hot pepper sauce
3 cloves garlic, minced
1/4 t. salt
1/2 t. pepper
6 ears sweet corn, husked and
    kernels removed
4 red, yellow and/or green
    peppers, coarsely chopped
1/2 c. shredded Parmesan cheese
1 head romaine lettuce, cut
    crosswise into 1-inch pieces

In a jar with a tight-fitting lid, combine 1/3 cup oil, lemon juice, sauces, garlic, salt and pepper. Cover and shake well; set aside. Heat remaining oil in a large skillet over medium-high heat. Add corn; sauté for 5 minutes, or until corn is tender and golden, stirring often. Remove from heat; keep warm. Combine corn, peppers and cheese in a large bowl. Pour olive oil mixture over top; toss lightly to coat. Serve over lettuce. Makes 6 to 8 servings.

Sherri Cooper
Armada, MI

Whenever my father comes to visit, he always requests this salad. He usually stops by the local vegetable stand on his way and picks up fresh ears of corn...just for this salad!

Mustard & Thyme Potato Salad

2 baking potatoes
1 to 2 T. red wine vinegar,
   divided
1 c. mayonnaise
2 T. plus 2 t. Dijon mustard
1 t. fresh thyme, minced, or
   1/2 t. dried thyme
pepper to taste
Garnish: 2 sprigs fresh thyme

Pierce potatoes with a fork; bake at
400 degrees for 45 minutes, or until
tender. When still warm but cool
enough to handle, remove and
discard skins. Cut into bite-size
pieces. Transfer potatoes to a
medium glass bowl. While potatoes
are still warm, lightly drizzle with
vinegar. Fold potatoes over and
lightly drizzle again. Gently fold once
more; set aside. In a small bowl,
combine mayonnaise, mustard,
thyme and pepper. Pour over
potatoes. Fold until evenly coated.
Transfer to a serving bowl; garnish
with thyme. Serve warm or chilled.
Serves 4 to 6.

151

Cinde Shields
Issaquah, WA

One creamy bite of potato
salad brings back cherished
memories of family reunions
in the park, summertime pool
parties and my grandmother's
busy kitchen.

Sunny Quinoa Salad

2 c. quinoa, uncooked
2-1/2 c. chicken broth
4 green onions, thinly sliced
1/2 c. golden raisins, chopped
2 T. rice vinegar
1/2 c. orange juice
1 t. orange zest
2 T. olive oil
1/4 t. ground cumin
1 cucumber, peeled and chopped
1/2 c. fresh flat-leaf parsley,
    chopped
salt and pepper to taste

Rinse quinoa under cold water until water runs clear. In a saucepan, bring chicken broth to a boil. Add quinoa; return to a boil. Cover and simmer until quinoa has fully expanded, about 20 to 25 minutes. Remove from heat; fluff with a fork. In a large bowl, combine quinoa and remaining ingredients; mix well. Cover and chill before serving. Serves 6 to 8.

JoAnn
With its bright flavors, this good-for-you salad makes a yummy lunch!

White Bean & Tomato Salad

15-oz. can cannellini beans,
  drained and rinsed
2 zucchini or yellow squash,
  diced
1 pt. cherry tomatoes, halved
1/2 c. red onion, chopped
3 T. olive oil
2 T. lemon juice
1/4 c. fresh cilantro, chopped

Combine all ingredients in a large
bowl. Cover and refrigerate. Let
stand at room temperature 20 to
30 minutes before serving.
Makes 6 servings.

153

Denise Neal
Castle Rock, CO
I got this delicious recipe
while on vacation in England.
We love it! If you can't get
cannellini beans, navy beans
will work fine.

A Little Different Macaroni Salad

16-oz. pkg. elbow macaroni,
  cooked
4 carrots, peeled and grated
1 sweet onion, chopped
1/2 c. red pepper, chopped
1/2 c. green pepper, chopped
2 c. mayonnaise
14-oz. can sweetened condensed
  milk
1/4 to 1/2 c. sugar
1/2 c. white vinegar
salt and pepper to taste

Combine macaroni, carrots, onion
and peppers in a large bowl. In a
separate bowl, whisk together
mayonnaise, condensed milk, sugar
and vinegar. Pour over macaroni and
vegetables. Season with salt and pepper.
Chill at least 8 hours to allow dressing
to thicken. Mix well before serving.
Makes 8 to 10 servings.

Wanda Wilson
Hamilton, GA

Sweetened condensed milk
is the secret ingredient!

Spicy Cabbage-Apple Slaw

2 c. shredded green and red
   cabbage mix
2 c. Red Delicious apples, cored
   and chopped
1/2 c. celery, chopped
2 T. walnuts, chopped and
   toasted
2 T. golden raisins
1/2 c. plain yogurt
2 T. apple juice
1 T. honey
1/2 t. cinnamon

In a large serving bowl, combine
cabbage mix, apples, celery, nuts
and raisins; toss well. Combine
remaining ingredients in a small
bowl, stirring well. Pour yogurt
mixture over cabbage mixture; toss
well. Cover and chill for at least
30 minutes before serving. Makes
8 servings.

Edie DeSpain
Logan, UT

We really like the
crunchiness of this salad
that comes from the cabbage,
apples, celery and walnuts...
yum! It goes well with
pork dishes.

German Green Beans

2 14-1/2 oz. cans green beans,
   drained
15-1/4 oz. can corn, drained
1 t. seasoned salt
1 T. onion powder
1 clove garlic, minced
1 T. vinegar
4 to 5 T. olive oil
4 to 5 carrots, peeled and grated
1/2 t. dill weed
1/2 t. dried oregano
1/4 t. dried tarragon
5 slices bacon, crisply cooked
   and crumbled

In a large serving bowl, mix together
all ingredients except bacon. Cover
and refrigerate overnight, stirring
occasionally. Top with bacon and
serve at room temperature. Makes 4 to
6 servings.

Patricia Taylor
Wellsville, PA

My family loves this
so much, there's never
any left over!

Hot & Sweet Coleslaw

8 c. green cabbage, shredded
1 c. red cabbage, shredded
4 carrots, peeled and shredded
1 yellow onion, grated
1/2 c. low-fat mayonnaise
2 T. mustard
2 t. cider vinegar
1/4 c. sugar
1 t. pepper
1/4 t. cayenne pepper
Optional: salt and additional
    pepper to taste

157

In a large bowl, toss together
vegetables. In a separate bowl,
whisk together mayonnaise, mustard,
vinegar, sugar and peppers. Toss
mayonnaise mixture with cabbage
mixture; season with salt and
additional pepper, if desired. Cover
and refrigerate overnight before
serving. Makes 10 to 12 servings.

Karen Christiansen
Glenview, IL

My husband, who doesn't
care for salads with a lot
of mayonnaise, enjoys this
slaw along with pulled
pork sandwiches.

Fruit Harvest Salad

32-oz. container vanilla yogurt
8-oz. pkg. cream cheese, softened
1/2 c. sugar
1/4 c. plus 1/3 c. brown sugar,
 packed and divided
1 t. vanilla extract
1 lb. seedless green grapes
1 lb. seedless red grapes
2 Gala apples, cored and diced
2 Granny Smith apples, cored
 and diced
1/2 c. sliced almonds
1/3 c. sweetened dried cranberries
15-oz. can mandarin oranges,
 drained
Optional: whipped cream

In a blender on medium speed, mix
yogurt and cream cheese until smooth.
Pour mixture into a large bowl. Stir in
sugar, 1/4 cup brown sugar and vanilla.
Add grapes, apples and almonds; toss
until coated. Cover and refrigerate
one hour. Uncover and smooth top of
salad. Top with cranberries, oranges
and whipped cream, if using. Sprinkle
with remaining brown sugar. Makes 15
to 20 servings.

Shanna Painter
Medicine Hat, Ontario

I love making this salad
with my young daughter.
Those who watch their sugar
will be happy to know
calorie-free sweeteners
work just as well!

Chicken & Rice Salad

3 T. red wine vinegar
1-1/2 T. extra-virgin olive oil
1/4 t. pepper
1 clove garlic, minced
2 c. long-grain rice, cooked
1-1/2 c. cooked chicken breast,
   diced
1/2 c. jarred roasted red peppers,
   drained and diced
1/2 c. Kalamata olives, pitted
   and halved
1/4 c. fresh chives, chopped
1/4 c. fresh basil, chopped
1/4 c. fresh oregano, chopped
14-oz. can artichokes, drained
   and diced
4-oz. pkg. crumbled feta cheese

159

In a small bowl, whisk together
vinegar, olive oil, pepper and garlic.
Set aside. In a separate bowl,
combine rice and remaining
ingredients except cheese. At serving
time, drizzle vinegar mixture over
salad; sprinkle with cheese. Makes
4 servings.

Francie Stutzman
North Fort Myers, FL

This dish is
scrumptious...I hope
you'll try it!

Roasted Veggie Tortellini Salad

20-oz. pkg. refrigerated 6-cheese
    tortellini pasta
1 red pepper, thinly sliced
3/4 c. red onion, thinly sliced
1/2 lb. asparagus, trimmed and
    cut into 1-1/2 inch pieces
salt and pepper to taste
2 T. olive oil, divided
1 zucchini, diced
7-oz. container basil pesto

Cook pasta according to package
directions; drain, rinse with cold water
and set aside. In a bowl, combine red
pepper, onion and asparagus. Season
with salt and pepper and toss with one
tablespoon olive oil. Arrange red
pepper mixture in a single layer on a
baking sheet. Bake at 450 degrees for
10 to 12 minutes. Remove from baking
sheet and set aside. Season zucchini
with salt and pepper; toss with
remaining olive oil. Arrange in a single
layer on a baking sheet. Bake for 5 to
7 minutes, until tender but not brown.
Combine roasted vegetables, cooked
tortellini and pesto in a large bowl.
Chill for at least one hour; serve
chilled. Makes 8 servings.

Christy Cox
Bristow, VA

This is a must for any
gathering! Look for the
tortellini and pesto in
the dairy or refrigerated
Italian food case.

11-Layer Garden in a Bowl

3 c. mayonnaise
2/3 c. sugar
2 10-oz. pkgs. mixed salad
    greens
1 lb. bacon, crisply cooked and
    crumbled
1 red onion, diced
10-oz. pkg. frozen peas, thawed
1 green pepper, diced
2 c. cauliflower flowerets
2 c. broccoli flowerets
1 c. sliced mushrooms
1 c. shredded Cheddar cheese
1 c. cherry tomatoes, halved
1 T. Italian seasoning

161

In a bowl, mix mayonnaise and
sugar until blended; set aside. Layer
half the salad greens in a large serving
bowl or 13"x9" glass baking pan.
Layer with half the mayonnaise
mixture, half the remaining
ingredients except tomatoes and
seasoning. Repeat layers. Top with
tomatoes and sprinkle with
seasoning. Cover and refrigerate
2 hours before serving. Makes
8 servings.

Nola Coons
Gooseberry Patch

This farm-fresh salad is for
those occasions when seven
layers just won't do!

Shrimp Tossed Salad

Amy Bleich
Jacksonville, FL

A simply scrumptious
mix that's super for
hot summer days!

1 head lettuce, torn
9-oz. pkg. baby spinach
3 c. coleslaw mix
8-oz. can sliced water chestnuts,
    drained
1/4 to 1/2 c. golden raisins
1/4 to 1/2 c. sweetened dried
    cranberries
1/2 red pepper, very thinly sliced
2-lb. pkg. frozen cooked shrimp,
    thawed
1 carrot, peeled
1/2 c. chow mein noodles
Optional: chopped fresh dill
Garnish: sweet-and-sour salad
    dressing

In a large serving bowl, arrange half
each of lettuce, spinach and coleslaw
mix. Top with half each of water
chestnuts, raisins and cranberries.
Layer with remaining lettuce, spinach
and coleslaw mix. Arrange red peppers
around the edge of the salad. Arrange
shrimp inside the pepper ring. Using a
vegetable peeler, make carrot curls;
arrange in center of bowl. Sprinkle
with remaining water chestnuts, raisins
and cranberries. Just before serving,
top with chow mein noodles. If
desired, sprinkle dill over the shrimp.
Serve with salad dressing. Serves 6.

Peppy 4-Bean Salad

14-1/2 oz. can green beans, drained
14-1/2 oz. can yellow beans, drained
15-1/2 oz. can kidney beans, drained
16-oz. can lima beans, drained
14-1/2 oz. can sliced carrots, drained
1 green pepper, chopped
1 red onion, chopped
1 c. celery, chopped
1/2 c. vinegar
1/2 c. water
1/2 c. oil
2 c. sugar
1 t. celery seed
1 t. salt

163

Mix together all beans and vegetables in a large bowl; set aside. In a separate bowl, whisk together remaining ingredients; toss with bean mixture. Cover and refrigerate for at least 24 hours. Makes 10 to 12 servings.

Debi DeVore
New Philadelphia, OH

This is my mom's recipe...
we enjoy it at all our
family cookouts.

Pasta Taco Salad

3 c. rotini pasta, uncooked
1 lb. ground beef
1-1/4 oz. pkg. taco seasoning mix
7 c. lettuce, torn
2 tomatoes, chopped
2 c. shredded Cheddar cheese
2 c. nacho-flavored tortilla chips,
  crushed

Cook pasta according to package directions; drain and rinse in cold water. Meanwhile, brown beef in a skillet; drain. Add taco seasoning and cook according to package directions. In a large bowl, combine pasta, beef and Dressing; toss until coated. Add lettuce, tomatoes and cheese. Toss to combine. Sprinkle with tortilla chips. Makes 12 to 14 servings.

Dressing:

1-1/4 c. mayonnaise
3 T. milk
3-3/4 t. cider vinegar
3-3/4 t. sugar
1 T. dry mustard

Whisk together all ingredients.

Lisa Seckora
Chippewa Falls, WI
Great at potlucks and family gatherings...everyone loves this salad with a kick!

Chilled Apple & Cheese Salad

3-oz. pkg. lemon gelatin mix
1 c. boiling water
3/4 c. cold water
2/3 c. red apple, cored and
    finely chopped
1/3 c. shredded Cheddar cheese
1/4 c. celery, chopped

In a bowl, dissolve gelatin in boiling water. Stir in cold water; chill until partially set. Fold in remaining ingredients. Pour into a 3-cup mold. Cover and chill 3 hours, or until firm. Unmold onto a serving plate. Makes 6 servings.

165

Melody Taynor
Everett, WA

As a girl, I was convinced that I didn't like gelatin salads. But when my Aunt Clara served this at an anniversary party, I found I had been mistaken!

Blueberry-Chicken Salad

2 c. chicken breast, cooked
  and cubed
3/4 c. celery, chopped
1/2 c. red pepper, diced
1/2 c. green onions, thinly sliced
2 c. blueberries, divided
6-oz. container lemon yogurt
3 T. mayonnaise
1/2 t. salt
Garnish: Bibb lettuce

Combine chicken and vegetables in a
large bowl. Gently stir in 1-1/2 cups
blueberries; reserve remaining berries.
In a separate bowl, blend remaining
ingredients except lettuce. Drizzle over
chicken mixture and gently toss to coat.
Cover and refrigerate 30 minutes.
Spoon salad onto lettuce-lined plates.
Top with reserved blueberries. Makes
4 servings.

Debi DeVore
New Philadelphia, OH
Fresh blueberries and lemony
yogurt add a fresh spin to
the usual chicken salad.

Pizza Salad

1 head iceberg lettuce, torn
1 c. sliced pepperoni
1 c. shredded mozzarella cheese
1 c. shredded Cheddar cheese
1 green pepper, chopped
1/2 c. sliced black olives
1/2 c. sliced mushrooms
1/2 c. red onion, sliced

Toss together all ingredients in a
large bowl. Toss with Pizza Dressing
at serving time. Serves 6.

Pizza Dressing:

1 c. pizza sauce
1/2 c. oil
1/4 c. red wine vinegar
1 t. sugar
1/2 t. salt
1 t. dried oregano
1/8 t. pepper
1/4 t. garlic powder

In a screw-top jar, combine all
ingredients; cover and shake well.

167

Karen Curnutt
Wichita, KS

We love pizza, so I came up
with this salad as a way to
enjoy it in a different form.
When I take it to potlucks,
everyone always wants
the recipe.

Black Cherry & Cranberry Salad

8-oz. can crushed pineapple
1/4 c. water
3-oz. pkg. black cherry gelatin mix
16-oz. can whole-berry cranberry
    sauce
1 c. celery, chopped
1 c. chopped walnuts
1/4 c. lemon juice

In a saucepan over medium heat, mix undrained pineapple and water. Heat to boiling; add gelatin mix and stir until gelatin is dissolved. Add remaining ingredients and stir well. Transfer to a 6-cup serving dish. Chill in refrigerator for 4 hours, or until firm. Makes 8 servings.

Leigh Ellen Eades
Summersville, WV

I remember my mother making this salad for Thanksgiving and Christmas when I was a child. Now, it's at the top of my own holiday menus!

Seafood Salad for a Crowd

3 8-oz. pkgs. cooked frozen
shrimp, thawed
2 lbs. imitation crabmeat, cut
into bite-size pieces
4 cucumbers, peeled and diced
6 tomatoes, diced
1 bunch green onions, chopped
1 head lettuce, chopped
4 avocados, halved, pitted
and diced
seasoned salt with onion &
garlic to taste
2 16-oz. pkgs. shredded
Colby Jack cheese
Garnish: ranch salad dressing

169

In a large bowl, toss together all
ingredients except cheese and salad
dressing. Divide salad into individual
bowls; top with cheese and salad
dressing. Serves 15.

Viola Travis
Donaldson, AR

I always set aside a
container of this refreshing
salad for my father...he
gets mad if I don't!

Layered Caribbean Chicken Salad

3 c. romaine lettuce, shredded
2 c. cooked chicken, cubed
1 c. shredded Monterey Jack cheese
15-1/2 oz. can black beans, drained
   and rinsed
1-1/2 c. mango, halved, pitted
   and cubed
1/2 c. plum tomatoes, chopped
1 c. shredded Cheddar cheese
1/2 c. green onions, thinly sliced
1/2 c. cashews, chopped

In a large clear glass serving bowl, layer all salad ingredients in order listed, except cashews. Spoon Dressing evenly over salad; sprinkle cashews over top. Makes 6 servings.

Dressing:

6-oz. container piña colada yogurt
2 T. lime juice
1 t. Caribbean jerk seasoning

In a small bowl, mix all ingredients together until well blended.

Laurel Perry
Loganville, GA

This is a wonderful way to use rotisserie chicken from the deli. You won't believe how yummy the dressing is!

Lucy's Sausage Salad

14-oz. pkg. mini smoked beef
   sausages, divided
1 t. canola oil
1 c. corn
15-1/2 oz. can black beans,
   drained and rinsed
1 T. canned jalapeño pepper,
   seeded and minced
1 c. red pepper, chopped
Garnish: fresh cilantro sprigs

Measure out half the sausages; set
aside for a future use. Slice
remaining sausages into 3 pieces
each. In a skillet, sauté sausages in
oil over medium heat until lightly
golden; drain. In a large bowl,
combine corn, beans, jalapeño and
red pepper. Stir in sausage. Toss with
Dressing; garnish with cilantro.
Serves 4.

Dressing:

3 T. low-fat plain yogurt
3 T. low-fat sour cream
1/4 c. picante sauce
1/2 c. fresh cilantro, chopped
salt and pepper to taste

Whisk together all ingredients.

171

Lucy Davis
Colorado Springs, CO
This deliciously different
salad may be made ahead and
chilled for one to two hours,
or served immediately.

Raspberry & Chicken Salad

1 c. white wine or chicken broth
1 c. water
4 boneless, skinless chicken breasts
1/3 c. olive oil
3 T. raspberry vinegar
1/2 t. Dijon mustard
salt and pepper to taste
10-oz. pkg. mixed salad greens
1 pt. raspberries

Combine wine or chicken broth and water in a saucepan over medium heat. Cover; bring to a boil. Reduce heat and add chicken. Cover and simmer 10 minutes, or until cooked through; drain. Let chicken cool and cut into 1/4-inch slices. Combine olive oil, vinegar, mustard, salt and pepper in a small screw-top jar; shake well. In a large bowl, toss salad greens with 1/3 of dressing. In a blender, blend 1/3 cup of raspberries and remaining dressing until smooth. Arrange salad on individual serving plates; top with chicken and remaining raspberries. Drizzle with dressing; serve immediately. Serves 4.

Rogene Rogers
Bemidji, MN

We can't wait for raspberry season so we can pick basketfuls ourselves! I like to serve this salad with fresh-baked muffins.

Lemon-Dill Chopped Salad

2 romaine lettuce hearts,
    chopped
1 c. cherry tomatoes, quartered
1 cucumber, peeled and cubed
3/4 c. baby carrots, cut in
    1/4-inch coins
1/2 c. crumbled feta cheese

In a large bowl, combine lettuce,
tomatoes, cucumber, carrots and
cheese. Cover and refrigerate. To
serve, toss with Dressing. Serves 4.

Dressing:

juice of 1 lemon
2 T. white wine vinegar
1 T. honey
2 T. fresh dill, chopped
1/4 t. salt
1/8 t. pepper
1/3 c. olive oil
1 apple, cored and coarsely
    grated

Whisk together lemon juice, vinegar,
honey, dill, salt and pepper. Slowly
whisk in oil in a thin stream; stir in
apple. Cover and refrigerate at least
2 hours.

173

Shirl Parsons
Cape Carteret, NC
This wonderful side dish
recipe was given to me by
a dear friend.

Scrumptious Chicken Sandwiches

1 egg, beaten
1 c. milk
4 to 6 boneless, skinless chicken
  breasts
1 c. all-purpose flour
2-1/2 T. powdered sugar
1 T. kosher salt
1/2 t. pepper
Optional: 1/8 t. allspice
oil for frying
4 to 6 hamburger buns, split
  and lightly toasted
Garnish: mayonnaise, dill
  pickle slices

Mix egg and milk together in an 11"x7" baking pan. Place chicken in pan, turn to coat and refrigerate for one hour. In a bowl, combine flour, sugar and spices. In a heavy skillet, heat one inch of oil to 400 degrees. Working in batches of 3, drain chicken, reserving egg mixture, and lightly dredge in flour mixture. Dip back into egg mixture, then into flour mixture again. Place very carefully into hot oil. Fry for 8 to 10 minutes, until done on both sides and juices run clear. Drain chicken on a wire rack. Assemble sandwiches on toasted buns and garnish as desired. Makes 4 to 6.

Sandy Carpenter
Washington, WV

These taste so much like
a popular restaurant's
sandwiches but cost
much less!

Scott's Ham & Pear Sandwiches

8 slices sourdough bread
4 slices Swiss cheese
1-1/4 lbs. sliced deli ham
15-oz. can pear halves, drained
  and thinly sliced

Spread each bread slice with a thin layer of Spiced Butter. On each of 4 slices, place one slice of cheese; layer evenly with ham and pears. Top with remaining bread slices and press together gently. Spread the outside of the sandwiches with Spiced Butter. Heat a large skillet over medium-high heat and cook until crisp and golden, about 5 minutes on each side. Makes 4 sandwiches.

Spiced Butter:

1 c. butter, softened
2 t. pumpkin pie spice
1 t. ground coriander
1 t. ground ginger
1 t. salt

Combine all ingredients until smooth and evenly mixed.

175

Kathy Majeske
Denver, PA

My brother, who is an amazing cook, gave me this recipe. The spiced butter makes it especially crispy and good!

Tuna Panini

12-oz. can tuna, drained
1 onion, chopped
4 to 6 dill pickle spears, chopped
1/2 to 3/4 c. carrot, peeled,
  shredded and chopped
3/4 to 1 c. shredded mozzarella
  cheese
mayonnaise to taste
1 T. olive oil
8 slices multi-grain bread, toasted
1 tomato, sliced

In a bowl, mix tuna, onion, pickles,
carrot, cheese and mayonnaise. In a
panini press or skillet, heat olive oil
over medium heat until hot. For each
sandwich, top one slice of toasted bread
with tuna mixture, 2 slices of tomato
and second slice of bread. Place
sandwich in a panini press or skillet;
heat one to 2 minutes, or until cheese
is melted. Makes 4 sandwiches.

Mary Stratton
Abington, MA

This is a quick recipe
that's perfect whenever
time is short and tummies

Louisiana Sausage Sandwiches

19.76-oz. pkg. Italian pork
    sausage links
1 green pepper, sliced into
    bite-size pieces
1 onion, sliced into bite-size
    pieces
8-oz. can tomato sauce
1/8 t. pepper
6 hoagie rolls, split

In a large skillet, brown sausage links
over medium heat. Cut into 1/2-inch
slices; place in a slow cooker. Stir in
remaining ingredients except rolls.
Cover and cook on low setting for
8 hours. Spoon into rolls with a
slotted spoon. Makes 6 sandwiches.

177

Dana Cunningham
Lafayette, LA

After working the county fair
one year with a friend, I
learned how to make these
sandwiches like a pro!

Baked Filled Sandwiches

1 loaf frozen bread dough, thawed
2 T. mayonnaise-type salad
  dressing
1/2 T. dried, minced onion
3/4 t. Italian seasoning
8 slices Swiss cheese
10 slices deli honey ham
10 slices deli roast turkey
1 egg, beaten
1 t. water
Garnish: sesame seed

On a floured surface, roll dough into a 14-inch by 12-inch rectangle. Spread with salad dressing; sprinkle with onion and seasoning. Make ten, 1-1/2 inch cuts on each long edge of the dough. Layer dough alternately with cheese, ham and turkey, ending with turkey. Criss-cross the cut strips over the top of the meat; place on an ungreased baking sheet and set aside. Combine egg and water; brush over dough. Sprinkle with sesame seed; let rise for 30 minutes. Bake at 350 degrees for 45 minutes to one hour, until golden. Slice to serve. Serves 8.

Elaine Wilcox
Austin, MN

This recipe was a customer favorite at the Gingerbread House, the restaurant my sister and I owned together.

BBQ Chicken Calzones

12-oz. tube refrigerated
   pizza dough
3 c. cooked chicken, diced
1 c. barbecue sauce
1 c. shredded mozzarella cheese
1 egg, beaten
1 t. water

179

On a floured surface, roll dough
to 1/2-inch thickness; cut into
2 rectangles and place on ungreased
baking sheets. In a bowl, combine
chicken and barbecue sauce. For
each calzone, spoon half the chicken
mixture onto one half of the dough.
Top with half the cheese. Fold over
dough and seal the edges. Mix
together egg and water. Use a pastry
brush to brush egg mixture over each
calzone; use a knife to cut 3 slits in
the tops. Bake at 400 degrees for
25 minutes, or until golden.
Makes 4 servings.

Jill Ross
Gooseberry Patch

With a recipe this easy,
it's a pleasure to have
my children lend a hand
in the kitchen!

Grilled Chicken & Zucchini Wraps

4 boneless, skinless chicken breasts
4 to 6 zucchini, sliced lengthwise
    into 1/4-inch thick slices
olive oil
salt and pepper to taste
1/2 c. ranch salad dressing, divided
8 10-inch whole-grain flour
    tortillas
8 leaves lettuce
Garnish: shredded Cheddar cheese

Brush chicken and zucchini with olive oil; sprinkle with salt and pepper. Grill chicken over medium-high heat for 5 minutes. Turn chicken over; add zucchini to grill. Grill 5 minutes longer, or until chicken juices run clear and zucchini is tender. Slice chicken into strips; set aside. For each wrap, spread one tablespoon salad dressing on a tortilla. Top with a lettuce leaf, 1/2 cup chicken and 3 to 4 slices of zucchini. Sprinkle with cheese; roll up. Makes 8 servings.

Teresa Willett
Thorold, Ontario

These wraps are a huge hit with my family...even my son who claims he doesn't like zucchini!

The Ultimate Shrimp Sandwich

3/4 lb. cooked shrimp, chopped
1/4 c. green pepper, chopped
1/4 c. celery, chopped
1/4 c. cucumber, chopped
1/4 c. tomato, diced
1/4 c. green onion, chopped
1/4 c. mayonnaise
Optional: hot pepper sauce
   to taste
6 split-top rolls, split and
   lightly toasted
2 T. butter, softened
1 c. lettuce, shredded

181

In a bowl, combine shrimp,
vegetables and mayonnaise; toss well.
Set aside. Spread rolls evenly with
butter; divide lettuce among rolls.
Top with shrimp mixture. Serves 6.

Karen Pilcher
Burleson, TX

Treat your family to this
scrumptious recipe. It also
makes a satisfying appetizer
when served on crackers.

Chicken Quesadillas El Grande

3 to 4-lb. deli roast chicken,
 shredded
3 T. salsa
salt and pepper to taste
1 onion, cut into strips
1 green pepper, cut into strips
3 T. olive oil
15-oz. can refried beans
8 10-inch flour tortillas
6-oz. pkg. shredded
 Mexican-blend cheese
Garnish: shredded lettuce, diced
 tomatoes, diced red onion,
 sour cream, guacamole,
 additional salsa

In a bowl, stir together chicken, salsa,
salt and pepper; set aside. In a skillet
over medium heat, cook onion and
pepper in oil until crisp-tender;
remove to a bowl. Evenly spread
refried beans onto 4 tortillas. For each
quesadilla, place one tortilla, bean-side
up, in a skillet coated with non-stick
vegetable spray. Top with a quarter of
chicken, onion mixture and cheese.
Place a plain tortilla on top. Cook over
medium heat until layers start to warm,
about 2 minutes. Flip over and cook
until tortilla is crisp and filling is hot.
Cut each quesadilla into wedges and
garnish as desired. Serves 4.

Michelle Papp
Rutherford, NJ

I just whipped this up
one afternoon for a quick
lunch and it was a
hit...so satisfying!

Buffalo Chicken Sandwich

6 boneless chicken breasts
1 onion, chopped
6 stalks celery, chopped
2 to 3 T. olive oil
1/2 c. all-purpose flour
Optional: 1 t. seasoning salt
17-1/2 oz. bottle buffalo
  wing sauce
6 soft buns, split
Garnish: ranch or blue cheese
  salad dressing, crumbled blue
  cheese, additional wing sauce

183

Flatten chicken breasts to 1/4-inch thin between pieces of wax paper; set aside. In a skillet over medium-low heat, sauté onion and celery in oil until tender. In a shallow bowl, combine flour and seasoning salt, if using. Dredge chicken pieces in flour mixture. Add chicken on top of onion mixture in pan. Cook for 5 minutes; flip chicken and cook an additional 5 minutes. Add buffalo wing sauce to pan. Cover; increase heat to medium, and cook 5 to 7 minutes, until chicken juices run clear. Serve on buns; garnish as desired. Makes 6 sandwiches.

Susan Buetow
Du Quoin, IL

Besides looking tasty, this sandwich is very easy to make. It's my go-to recipe when hubby is having buddies over!

Cheesy Zucchini Joes

2 T. butter
2 zucchini, halved and sliced
1/8 t. red pepper flakes
1/8 t. garlic powder
salt and pepper to taste
1 c. marinara or spaghetti sauce
1 to 2 c. shredded mozzarella
   cheese
4 6-inch sub rolls, split

Melt butter in a skillet over medium heat. Fry zucchini in butter until golden and slightly tender. Add seasonings. Stir in sauce. Cook and stir until sauce is heated through. For each sandwich, spoon a generous amount of zucchini mixture onto bottom half of bun. Sprinkle with cheese and replace bun top. Wrap sandwiches individually in aluminum foil. Place on a baking sheet and bake at 350 degrees for 15 minutes, or until heated through and cheese is melted. Makes 4 sandwiches.

Kim McLaughlin
Cambridge, OH

My grandma planted lots of zucchini. We always joked that she would serve zucchini in every dish possible!

Game-Day Sandwich

3 T. mayonnaise
1 T. mustard
1-lb. round loaf Hawaiian-style
  bread
1/4 lb. sliced deli turkey
1/4 lb. sliced deli roast beef
3 slices Swiss cheese
3 lettuce leaves
1/4 lb. sliced deli ham
6 slices bacon, crisply cooked
3 slices Cheddar cheese
6 slices tomato

185

Mix mayonnaise and mustard
together. Cut bread horizontally into
3 layers. Spread half of mayonnaise
mixture on the bottom layer. Add
turkey, roast beef, Swiss cheese and
lettuce. Cover with middle bread
layer; spread with remaining
mayonnaise mixture. Add ham,
bacon, Cheddar cheese and tomato.
Top with remaining bread layer.
Cut into 6 to 8 slices. Makes 6 to
8 servings.

Yvonne Coleman
Statesville, NC
My husband loves this
sandwich and requests it
on his birthday. It has
something to please everyone.

Backyard Big South-of-the-Border Burgers

4-oz. can chopped green chiles,
   drained
1/4 c. picante sauce
12 round buttery crackers, crushed
4-1/2 t. chili powder
1 T. ground cumin
1/2 t. smoke-flavored cooking
   sauce
1/2 t. salt
1/2 t. pepper
2 lbs. lean ground beef
1/2 lb. ground pork sausage
6 slices Pepper Jack cheese
6 sesame seed hamburger buns,
   split
Garnish: lettuce leaves, sliced
   tomato

In a large bowl, combine first
8 ingredients. Crumble beef and
sausage over mixture and mix well.
Form into 6 patties. Grill, covered,
over medium heat for 5 to 7 minutes
on each side, or until no longer pink.
Top with cheese. Grill until cheese is
melted. Grill buns, cut-side down, for
one to 2 minutes, or until toasted.
Serve burgers on buns, garnished as
desired. Makes 6 servings.

Paula Marchesi
Lenhartsville, PA

Every time I bite into
a scrumptious, juicy
burger cooked on an outside
grill, I'm a kid again,
at our picnic table with
family & friends.

Seaside Salmon Buns

14-oz. can salmon, drained
   and flaked
1/4 c. green pepper, chopped
1 T. onion, chopped
2 t. lemon juice
1/2 c. mayonnaise
6 hamburger buns, split
1/2 c. shredded Cheddar cheese
6 thick tomato slices

Mix salmon, pepper, onion, lemon
juice and mayonnaise. Pile salmon
mixture onto bottom bun halves;
sprinkle with cheese. Arrange
salmon-topped buns on an
ungreased baking sheet. Broil until
lightly golden and cheese is melted.
Top with tomato slices and remaining
bun halves. Serves 6.

187

Sharon Velenosi
Garden Grove, CA

For a real homestyle treat,
substitute fresh-baked
biscuits for the
hamburger buns.

Texas Steak Sandwiches

8 slices frozen Texas toast
1-1/2 lbs. deli roast beef, sliced
steak sauce to taste
8 slices provolone cheese
Optional: sliced green pepper and
  red onion, sautéed

Bake Texas toast on a baking sheet at
425 degrees for about 5 minutes per
side, until softened and lightly golden;
set aside. Warm roast beef in a skillet
over medium heat until most of the
juices have evaporated; stir in steak
sauce. Divide beef evenly among 4 toast
slices; top with cheese, pepper and
onion, if desired. Place beef-topped
toast and remaining toast on a baking
sheet; bake at 425 degrees until
cheese is melted. Combine to form
sandwiches. Makes 4 sandwiches.

Julie Horn
Chrisney, IN

My husband and I love these
hearty sandwiches. They're
super simple to make...when
guests drop by, I can whip
them up in no time.

Mexican Hot Dogs

8 hot dogs
8 slices bacon
8 hot dog buns
1 c. sour cream
1/2 c. onion, chopped
3/4 c. tomato, chopped
4-oz. can chopped jalapeño
   peppers, drained
Garnish: mustard and catsup

Pierce hot dogs with a fork 3 or 4 times. Wrap one slice of bacon around each hot dog. Over medium heat, grill or sauté on a griddle until bacon is lightly golden on all sides. Remove wire twist from hot dog bun bag. Microwave buns in bag for 30 to 45 seconds. Carefully remove buns from bag; cut open buns. Spread sour cream on both halves of each bun. Place bacon-wrapped hot dog in bun. Top with onion, tomato and jalapeños. Garnish with mustard and catsup. Makes 8.

189

**Leslie Limon
Yahualica, Mexico**

My hubby introduced me to these unbelievably good hot dogs. This is how they're made in his hometown in Mexico.

Mom's Slow-Cooker Mini Reubens

1/4 to 1/2 lb. deli corned beef, chopped
2 16-oz. pkgs. shredded Swiss cheese
8-oz. bottle Thousand Island salad dressing
32-oz. pkg. refrigerated sauerkraut, drained and chopped
Optional: 1 t. caraway seed
1 to 2 loaves party rye bread
Garnish: dill pickle slices

Put all ingredients except party rye and pickles in a slow cooker. Cover and cook on low setting for about 4 hours, or until mixture is hot and cheese is melted. Stir to blend well. To serve, arrange party rye slices and pickles on separate plates around slow cooker. Makes 10 to 12 servings.

Cheryl Breeden
North Platte, NE

This was always my mom's favorite recipe during football season...even if our team lost, dinner was always a winner!

Toasted Chicken Salad Bagels

6 c. cooked chicken, chopped
2 c. celery, chopped
1 c. almonds, chopped and
    toasted
1/4 c. lemon juice
1/4 c. onion, grated
1 t. salt
2 c. mayonnaise
1 c. shredded Cheddar cheese
12 bagels, sliced
2 c. potato chips, crushed

191

In a bowl, combine all ingredients
except bagels and chips. Spread
mixture on bottom halves of bagels.
Transfer bagels and tops to an
ungreased baking sheet. Broil for
3 to 5 minutes, until golden.
Sprinkle chips on chicken mixture.
Replace bagel tops. Makes
12 servings.

Kara McCreary
Wooster, OH

A crunchy twist on
traditional chicken
salad sandwiches.

Triple-Take Grilled Cheese

1 T. oil
8 slices sourdough bread
1/4 c. butter, softened and divided
4 slices American cheese
4 slices Muenster cheese
1/2 c. shredded sharp Cheddar
   cheese
Optional: 4 slices red onion,
   4 slices tomato, 1/4 c. chopped
   fresh basil

Heat oil in a skillet over medium heat. Spread 2 bread slices with one tablespoon butter; place one slice butter-side down on skillet. Layer one slice American, one slice Muenster and 2 tablespoons Cheddar cheese on bread. If desired, top with an onion slice, a tomato slice and one tablespoon basil. Place second buttered bread slice on top of sandwich in skillet. Reduce heat to medium-low. Cook until golden on one side, about 3 to 5 minutes; flip and cook until golden on the other side. Repeat with remaining ingredients. Makes 4 sandwiches.

Abigail Smith
Worthington, OH

Delicious in winter with a steaming bowl of tomato soup. And delicious in summer with produce fresh from the garden!

Chicken Tacos

2 T. olive oil
1 onion, chopped
2 T. garlic, minced
2 to 3 lbs. boneless, skinless
   chicken thighs or breasts, cut
   into bite-size pieces
10-oz. can diced tomatoes with
   green chiles
4-oz. can diced green chiles
1/8 to 1/4 t. hot pepper sauce
1 T. dried cilantro
salt and pepper to taste
12-oz. pkg. 6-inch corn tortillas
Garnish: shredded Cheddar
   cheese

193

Heat oil in a large skillet over
medium heat. Sauté onion and
garlic until tender. Add chicken and
cook through. Stir in remaining
ingredients except tortillas and
cheese; reduce heat. Stirring often,
simmer 8 to 10 minutes, until most
of the liquid is cooked out. Spoon
into tortillas and garnish with cheese.
Serves 6 to 8.

Katherine Jaworowski
Devine, TX
I made up this recipe and
know it's a real winner
because it's the one dish
I never have leftovers from!

Cheeseburger Roll-Ups

2 lbs. ground beef
3/4 c. soft bread crumbs
1/2 c. onion, minced
2 eggs, beaten
1-1/2 t. salt
1-1/2 t. pepper
12-oz. pkg. shredded Cheddar
   cheese
6 to 8 sandwich buns, split
Garnish: catsup, mustard
   and lettuce

In a large bowl, combine beef, bread crumbs, onion, eggs, salt and pepper; mix well. Pat out into an 18-inch by 14-inch rectangle on a piece of wax paper. Spread cheese over meat, leaving a 3/4-inch border around edges. Roll up jelly-roll fashion starting at short edge. Press ends to seal. Place on a lightly greased 15"x10" jelly-roll pan. Bake at 350 degrees for one hour, or until internal temperature on a meat thermometer reaches 160 degrees. Let stand at least 10 minutes before slicing. Slice and serve on buns; garnish as desired. Serves 6 to 8.

Kelly Alderson
Erie, PA

Made before we leave to go camping, these super-simple sandwiches disappear just as soon as our tent is set up!

Party-Time Lasagna Buns

4 French bread rolls
1 lb. ground beef
1.35-oz. pkg. onion or
   mushroom soup mix
1/4 t. dried oregano
1/4 t. dried basil
8-oz. can tomato sauce
3/4 c. cottage cheese
2 c. shredded mozzarella cheese,
   divided
1 egg, beaten

Slice the top off each roll and set aside. Hollow out the rolls. In a skillet over medium heat, brown beef; drain. Stir in soup mix, seasonings and tomato sauce. Simmer until heated through. In a bowl, mix cottage cheese, one cup mozzarella and egg. For each sandwich, spoon a layer of the beef mixture into the bottom of a bun. Spoon on a layer of cheese mixture and a layer of beef mixture. Top with remaining mozzarella. Replace bun top and wrap in aluminum foil. Place on a baking sheet and bake at 400 degrees for 30 minutes, or until cheese is melted. Makes 4 sandwiches.

195

Joyce Stath
Tell City, IN

Here's a hint to prevent the rolls from tearing...place them in the freezer for about an hour prior to slicing.

Yiayia's Chicken Pitas

1/2 c. plain yogurt
1/4 c. cucumber, finely chopped
1/2 t. dill weed
1/4 t. dried mint, crushed
4 pita bread rounds
4 lettuce leaves
2 c. cooked chicken, cubed
1 tomato, thinly sliced
1/3 c. crumbled feta cheese

In a small bowl, stir together yogurt, cucumber, dill weed and mint; set aside. For each sandwich, layer a pita with lettuce, chicken, tomato and cheese. Spoon yogurt mixture on top. Roll up pita and secure with a wooden toothpick. Serve immediately. Makes 4 servings.

Tori Willis
Champaign, IL

Though not exactly like my grandma's famous Greek sandwiches, they're pretty darn close!

All-American Sandwiches

1-1/2 T. olive oil
2 red onions, thinly sliced
3-1/2 T. red wine vinegar
6 c. arugula leaves, divided
3/4 c. mayonnaise
salt and pepper to taste
4 ciabatta rolls, halved
3/4 lb. thinly sliced smoked
    deli turkey
3/4 c. crumbled blue cheese

Heat oil in a skillet over medium-high heat. Add onions and sauté until soft and lightly golden. Remove from heat and stir in vinegar. Set aside. Chop enough arugula to equal one cup. Stir in mayonnaise; season with salt and pepper. Spread arugula mixture over cut sides of rolls. Divide turkey evenly among bottom halves of rolls. Top with cheese, onion mixture, remaining arugula leaves and top halves of rolls. Makes 4 sandwiches.

197

JoAnn
Celebrate summer with these yummy sandwiches...the blue cheese is scrumptious!

Annelle's Special Veggie Melts

1 c. sliced baby portabella
    mushrooms
1/4 c. olive oil
1 loaf focaccia bread, halved
    horizontally
15-oz. jar whole roasted red
    peppers, drained
1-1/2 t. Italian seasoning
1 c. shredded Fontina cheese

In a skillet over medium heat, sauté mushrooms in olive oil until tender. Place bread halves on an ungreased baking sheet. On one bread half, layer peppers, mushrooms and Italian seasoning. Top both halves evenly with cheese. Broil until lightly golden. Assemble sandwich and cut into 4 pieces. Makes 4 servings.

Amy Butcher
Columbus, GA

I'm lucky enough to live in a neighborhood with a corner bakery. Annelle, its owner, makes the best focaccia I've ever tasted!

Beef Stroganoff Sandwich

2 lbs. ground beef
1/2 c. onion, chopped
1/2 t. garlic powder
1 t. salt
1/2 t. pepper
1 loaf French bread, halved
    lengthwise
4 to 6 T. butter, softened
2 c. sour cream
2 tomatoes, diced
1 green pepper, diced
3 c. shredded Cheddar cheese

In a skillet over medium heat, brown beef and onion. Drain; stir in seasonings. Spread both halves of bread with butter; place butter-side up on an ungreased baking sheet. Remove skillet from heat; stir in sour cream. Spoon beef mixture onto bread; sprinkle with remaining ingredients. Bake at 350 degrees for 20 minutes, or until cheese is melted. If crisper bread is desired, bake a little longer. Slice into 3-inch portions to serve. Makes 6 servings.

Carol Blankenship
Hamilton, OH

My family just loves this open-face sandwich! I always make it for special occasions like family get-togethers. It's a great recipe.

Stuffed Bacon Cheeseburgers

1 lb. ground beef
1 T. garlic, minced
1 T. steak seasoning
1 T. dried parsley
1/2 t. paprika
1/2 t. onion powder
1 T. Worcestershire sauce
4 slices bacon, crisply cooked
   and cut in half
2 slices Cheddar cheese,
   cut into quarters
salt and pepper to taste
4 hamburger buns, split
Garnish: mustard, catsup,
   mayonnaise

In a bowl, mix beef, garlic, seasonings and Worcestershire sauce just until combined. Form into 8 thin patties. For each burger, place 2 pieces of bacon and 2 slices of cheese onto 4 patties. Top with another patty and seal edges. Sprinkle with salt and pepper. Grill over medium heat to desired doneness. Serve on buns, garnished as desired. Makes 4 servings.

Rebecca Reynoso
Ballwin, MO

What a wonderful surprise to discover bacon and cheese in the center of a juicy burger!

Famous Hidden Sandwich

1 slice rye bread
1 slice deli ham
1 slice Swiss cheese
1 slice deli turkey
1 c. lettuce, shredded
1/2 c. Russian or Thousand
  Island salad dressing
1 egg, hard-boiled, peeled
  and sliced
2 slices tomato
2 slices bacon, crisply cooked
Garnish: sweet pickle slices

201

Place bread slice on a plate. Layer with ham, cheese and turkey slices. Mound shredded lettuce on top. Cover with salad dressing. Top with egg slices and tomato slices; criss-cross bacon slices on top. Garnish with sweet pickle slices. Makes one sandwich.

Jennie Gist
Gooseberry Patch

I have fond memories of lunching at the old department store downtown with my best friend. This sandwich was a favorite... you'll need a knife and fork!

Kentucky Hot Browns

1/4 c. butter
1/4 c. all-purpose flour
2 c. milk
2 cubes chicken bouillon
16-oz. pkg. pasteurized process
    cheese spread, cubed
6 slices bread, toasted
12 slices deli turkey
6 slices deli ham
6 slices bacon, crisply cooked
6 slices tomato

Melt butter in a heavy saucepan over low heat. Stir in flour until smooth. Cook one minute, stirring constantly. Stir in milk and bouillon cubes. Cook until thick and bubbly. Add cheese and stir until smooth. Place toast slices in a buttered 13"x9" baking pan. Layer each with turkey and ham. Evenly spread cheese sauce over ham. Top each with bacon and tomato. Bake, uncovered, at 350 degrees for 3 to 5 minutes, until bubbly. Makes 6 servings.

Angie Stone
Argillite, KY

I learned to make these cheesy-good sandwiches when I was very young. They're a real favorite here in Kentucky.

Honey-Barbecued Pork

2 to 3-lb. pork roast
2 onions, chopped
12-oz. bottle barbecue sauce
1/4 c. honey
6 to 8 sandwich rolls, split

Place pork in a slow cooker. Add onions, barbecue sauce and honey. Cover and cook on low setting for 6 to 8 hours. Use 2 forks to shred roast; mix well. Serve on rolls. Makes 6 to 8 servings.

203

Carol Smith
West Lawn, PA

This slow-cooker recipe is my mom's. Try it on mini buns for sliders!

Farmhouse Honey Mustard ▶

1/4 c. mayonnaise
1/4 c. Dijon mustard
1/4 c. honey
1 T. mustard
1 T. white vinegar
1/8 t. paprika

Whisk together all ingredients in a small bowl. Cover and store in the refrigerator for up to one week. Makes about one cup.

Virginia Watson
Scranton, PA

There are so many ways to use this sweet-tangy mustard. You can spread it on sandwiches, drizzle over salads or spoon into a bowl for dipping chicken tenders...yum!

Bacon-Onion Croutons

6 slices French bread, crusts
   trimmed
2 T. bacon drippings
2 T. olive oil
1/2 t. onion powder
1 t. poppy seed
1/2 t. sesame seed, toasted

Cube bread; set aside. Heat
remaining ingredients in a skillet
over medium heat; stir in bread
cubes until well coated. Remove
from heat; spread mixture in a
single layer on an ungreased
15"x10" jelly-roll pan. Bake at
300 degrees until golden and crisp,
about 25 to 30 minutes. Let cool.
Store in an airtight container.
Makes about 2 cups.

205

**Nancy Wise
Little Rock, AR**

Why use store-bought
when homemade tastes
so much better?

Creamy Basil Salad Dressing

1 t. shallot, chopped
1 clove garlic, chopped
2/3 c. Greek yogurt
3 T. balsamic vinegar
1 T. lemon juice
3 T. olive oil
1/2 c. dried basil
salt and pepper to taste

Place all ingredients except salt and pepper in a food processor or blender. Proccess until smooth. Season with salt and pepper. Keep refrigerated. Makes about 1-1/2 cups.

Pat Minnich
El Cajon, CA
I grow my own basil and love this recipe. The dressing is so flavorful you would never guess it's low in fat!

Zesty Pita Crisps

6 T. sesame oil
1-1/2 t. ground cumin
salt to taste
3 pita rounds, split
Garnish: additional salt
  and cumin

In a small bowl, stir together oil, cumin and salt. Brush the cut sides of the pita rounds with oil mixture. Cut each round into 6 triangles. Arrange in a single layer in an ungreased 15"x10" jelly-roll pan. Bake at 350 degrees for 10 to 12 minutes, until golden. Toss warm crisps with additional salt and cumin; let cool. Serve immediately or store in an airtight container. Makes about 3 cups.

207

Brenda Smith
Delaware, OH

Oh-so simple! Pop these in the oven while the soup simmers on the stove and the salad is tossed.

Refrigerator Pickles

3 c. cucumbers, peeled and sliced
1 onion, thinly sliced
3/4 c. sugar
2/3 c. white vinegar
1/2 t. celery seed
1/2 t. mustard seed
1/4 t. salt

Mix cucumbers and onion in a glass or plastic bowl; set aside. Stir remaining ingredients together in a microwave-safe container. Microwave on high for 3 minutes, stirring after 2 minutes. Pour over cucumber mixture. Cover and refrigerate for 24 hours before serving to blend flavors. Keep refrigerated. Makes one quart.

Kay Barg
Sandy, UT

Super simple...a great recipe for first-time pickle makers.

Cheese & Garlic Croutons

1/4 c. butter
1/2 t. dried oregano
1/2 t. dried basil
1/2 t. celery salt
2 cloves garlic, minced
1 T. onion, minced
2 c. whole-wheat bread, cubed
2 T. grated Parmesan cheese

Heat butter in a large skillet. Add seasonings, garlic and onion; cook for about one minute to soften. Stir in bread cubes; sauté until golden and crisp. Toss with cheese until coated. Cool; store in an airtight container. Makes 2 cups.

209

Kendall Hale
Lynn, MA

These savory croutons are delicious sprinkled in a bowl of soup or tossed in a dinner salad.

Mom's Hot Bacon Dressing

4 slices bacon
2 T. sugar
2 T. all-purpose flour
1 egg, beaten
2 T. cider vinegar
1/4 c. water
3/4 c. milk

In a skillet over medium heat, cook bacon until crisp. Remove bacon and reserve drippings in skillet. In a small bowl, mix sugar, flour, egg and vinegar until smooth. Stir in water and milk and add to drippings. Crumble bacon and return to skillet. Cook over medium-low heat until thickened. More water or milk may be added until dressing reaches desired consistency. Serve warm. Store in the refrigerator for up to one week. Makes about 2 cups.

Jacqueline Kurtz
Wernersville, PA

My mom used to make this all the time to drizzle over fresh endive...it's a country classic. This dressing is very good added to homemade hot potato salad too.

Blue Cheese Cut-Out Crackers

1 c. all-purpose flour
7 T. butter, softened
7 T. crumbled blue cheese
1/2 t. dried parsley
1 egg yolk
1/8 t. salt
4 t. whipping cream
cayenne pepper to taste

Mix all ingredients together; let rest for 30 minutes. Roll dough out to about 1/8-inch thick. Use small cookie cutters to cut out crackers. Bake on ungreased baking sheets at 400 degrees for 8 to 10 minutes, just until golden. Let cool; remove carefully. Store in an airtight container. Makes 1-1/2 to 2 dozen.

211

Vickie

Delicate cheese wafers with a touch of hot pepper!

Lemony Sage Mayonnaise

2 c. mayonnaise
1/2 c. fresh sage, finely chopped,
   or 3 T. dried sage
2 T. lemon juice
1 T. plus 1 t. lemon zest
1 T. garlic, minced
1 t. pepper

Whisk together all ingredients. Cover
and store in the refrigerator for up to
one week. Makes about 2 cups.

Stacie Avner
Delaware, OH

Top sandwiches with
this spread...it's
packed with flavor!

Spicy Chili Crackers

16-oz. pkg. saltine crackers
1 c. olive oil
1-oz. pkg. ranch salad dressing
   mix
2 t. chili seasoning mix
1 t. garlic powder
Optional: cayenne pepper
   to taste

Place crackers in a large bowl;
set aside. Combine remaining
ingredients in a separate bowl and
stir to mix. Pour over crackers;
gently stir and let stand overnight.
May also be spread on a baking sheet
and baked at 250 degrees for 20 to
30 minutes. Store in an airtight
container. Makes 15 to 18 servings.

Gloria Robertson
Midland, TX

These savory crackers are
irresistible! Serve with a
bowl of soup or add to your
game-day buffet table.

Hamburger Stroganoff Casserole, page 270

Baked Chicken Jambalaya, page 269

Savory Rice Casserole, page 314

Taco-Filled Pasta Shells, page 245

101 Cozy Casseroles

Peg's Tomato-Bacon Pie, page 283

Warm & Wonderful Chicken Salad, page 295

Cheesy Vegetable Casserole, page 307

Here's one of our best collections of quick-fix and classic casseroles for any night of the week...there's nothing easier or more tasty than a hot & bubbly meal right from the oven.

Curry Chicken Casserole, page 277

Cabbage Roll Casserole, page 287

Scalloped Potatoes, page 304

Tips & Hints for Delicious Casseroles

★ A busy-day hint…if family members will be eating at different times, spoon casserole ingredients into individual ramekins for baking. Each person can enjoy their own fresh-from-the-oven mini casserole.

★ An old hometown tradition is "Never return a dish empty." After a get-together or potluck, gather up casserole dishes that have been left behind, fill them with home-baked goodies and return to their owners!

★ Casseroles spell comfort food, but what if the recipe is large and your family is small? Simple…just divide the casserole ingredients into two small dishes and freeze one for later!

★ To cut down on casserole prep time, stock up on pre-cut and peeled veggies available in the grocery produce aisle or salad bar.

★ A handy chart in case you don't have the exact size pan or dish called for:

13"x9" baking pan = 3-quart casserole dish
9"x9" baking pan = 2-quart casserole dish
8"x8" baking pan = 1-1/2 quart casserole dish

Pizza Potato Puff Casserole

1 lb. ground beef
1/4 c. onion, chopped
10-3/4 oz. can cream of
   mushroom soup
8-oz. can pizza sauce
12 to 15 slices pepperoni
1/2 c. green pepper, chopped
1 c. shredded mozzarella cheese
16-oz. pkg. frozen potato puffs

Brown beef and onion in a skillet over medium-high heat; drain. Stir in soup. Spoon beef mixture into an 8"x8" baking pan that has been lightly sprayed with non-stick vegetable spray. Spoon pizza sauce evenly over beef mixture; arrange pepperoni and green pepper over sauce. Sprinkle with cheese; arrange potato puffs over top. Cover with aluminum foil; bake at 375 degrees for 30 minutes. Uncover; bake an additional 15 to 20 minutes, until heated through. Serves 4.

217

Gladys Kielar
Perrysburg, OH

Friday night is pizza night at our house...sometimes our family enjoys this version for variety.

Pork Chop Potato Bake

1 T. oil
6 boneless pork chops
seasoned salt and pepper to taste
1 c. shredded Cheddar cheese,
    divided
10-3/4 oz. can cream of
    mushroom soup
1/2 c. milk
1/2 c. sour cream
28-oz. pkg. frozen diced
    potatoes with onions and
    peppers, thawed
1 to 2 T. onion soup mix

Heat oil in a skillet over medium-high heat. Season pork chops with salt and pepper; brown in oil for 5 minutes per side, until golden. In a bowl, combine 1/2 cup cheese and remaining ingredients. Spread cheese mixture in a greased 13"x9" baking pan. Arrange pork chops over top. Bake, covered, at 350 degrees for 40 minutes. Top with remaining cheese. Bake, uncovered, for an additional 10 minutes, or until cheese is melted. Serves 6.

Jackie Flood
Geneseo, NY
This is one of those dishes where the leftovers can taste even better!

Chicken Kiev Casserole

12-oz. pkg. wide egg noodles,
   uncooked
1/4 c. butter, softened
1 t. garlic powder
1 T. fresh parsley, chopped
1 deli roast chicken, cubed,
   divided and juices reserved
2 c. frozen peas, thawed
1 c. whipping cream
paprika to taste
Optional: additional fresh
   parsley

Cook noodles according to package
directions until just tender; drain
and set aside. In a bowl, combine
butter, garlic powder and parsley.
Use one teaspoon of butter mixture
to grease a 13"x9" baking pan. Layer
half the chicken, half the noodles and
all the peas; dot with half the
remaining butter mixture. Repeat
layers with remaining chicken,
noodles and butter mixture. Pour
reserved chicken juices and cream
over top; sprinkle with paprika.
Bake, uncovered, at 350 degrees for
30 minutes, or until hot and bubbly.
Sprinkle with parsley, if using.
Serves 6.

219

John Alexander
New Britain, CT

This savory, classic dish
is so good re-imagined
as a casserole.

Crustless Pizza Quiche

1/2 c. pepperoni, diced
8-oz. can sliced mushrooms,
    drained
5 eggs, beaten
3/4 c. milk
1/8 t. dried oregano
1/8 t. dried basil
8-oz. pkg. shredded mozzarella
    cheese

Layer pepperoni and mushrooms in
a greased 9" pie plate. In a bowl,
whisk together eggs, milk and
seasoning; pour over pepperoni and
mushrooms. Top with cheese. Bake,
uncovered, at 400 degrees for 20 to
25 minutes, until golden and heated
through. Serves 4 to 6.

Amy Hunt
Traphill, NC

This quiche goes well
with a salad for
a quick supper!

Easy Chicken Pot Pie

2 8-oz. cans chicken, drained
2 13-1/4 oz. cans mixed
   vegetables, drained
2 10-3/4 oz. cans cream of
   chicken soup
1 c. milk
salt and pepper to taste
8-oz. pkg. shredded Cheddar
   or Colby cheese, divided
12-oz. tube refrigerated biscuits

In a bowl, combine all ingredients
except cheese and biscuits. Transfer
to a greased 13"x9" baking pan; top
with 3/4 of cheese. Separate biscuits
and tear each into 4 to 5 pieces; place
on top of cheese. Sprinkle with
remaining cheese. Bake, uncovered,
at 350 degrees for 45 minutes, or
until biscuits are golden. Serves 4.

221

Lynne Gasior
Struthers, OH
This is also a great way
to use up leftover chicken
or a rotisserie chicken.

Ravioli Lasagna

1 lb. ground beef
1 onion, diced
26-oz. jar pasta sauce, divided
25-oz. pkg. frozen cheese ravioli,
   divided
1-1/2 c. shredded mozzarella
   cheese, divided

In a skillet over medium heat, brown beef with onion; drain. In a greased 11"x7" baking pan, layer one cup pasta sauce, half the frozen ravioli, half the beef mixture and half the cheese. Repeat layering with one cup pasta sauce and remaining ravioli and beef mixture. Add remaining pasta sauce. Bake, uncovered, at 425 degrees for 30 to 35 minutes. Top with remaining cheese and bake until melted, about 5 minutes. Serves 4 to 6.

Denise Moloney
Brooksville, FL

This super-simple dish was one of my mom's favorites...everytime I make it I think of her.

Hamburger Noodle Casserole

16-oz. pkg. wide egg noodles,
   uncooked
1-3/4 lbs. lean ground beef
1 onion, chopped
1 green pepper, chopped
1 t. salt
1 t. pepper
26-oz. can cream of mushroom
   soup
12-oz. pkg. shredded Cheddar
   cheese

Cook noodles according to package
directions. Drain; set aside.
Meanwhile, in a skillet over medium
heat, brown beef with onion, green
pepper, salt and pepper; drain.
Combine beef mixture, noodles
and soup. Pour into a greased
13"x9" baking pan; top with cheese.
Bake, uncovered, at 325 degrees for
10 to 15 minutes, until cheese is
melted and bubbly. Serves 6 to 8.

223

Gloria Kirkland
Pearson, GA

This is a quick & easy recipe
that uses basic ingredients,
comes together in a snap
and tastes so good.

Quick Tuna Casserole

2 6-oz. cans tuna, drained
10-3/4 oz. can cream of
   mushroom soup
3/4 c. milk
1 T. Worcestershire sauce
hot pepper sauce to taste
1 sleeve round buttery crackers,
   crushed

In a bowl, mix together all ingredients
except crackers; set aside. In a
greased 9"x9" baking pan, layer
one-third of crackers and top with
half of tuna mixture. Repeat layers;
top with remaining crackers and
more hot sauce, if desired. Bake,
uncovered, at 350 degrees for
30 minutes, or until hot and bubbly.
Serves 4.

Debbi Corlew
Colona, IL

I grew up eating this meal,
and it's still one of my
all-time favorites.

Gnocchi Casserole

1 lb. ground pork sausage
16-oz. pkg. frozen gnocchi
26-oz. jar pasta sauce
1-1/2 t. Italian seasoning
2 c. shredded mozzarella cheese,
    divided

Brown sausage in a skillet over medium heat; drain. Meanwhile, cook gnocchi according to package directions; drain. In a greased 2-quart casserole dish, combine all ingredients except one cup cheese. Bake, uncovered, at 350 degrees for 25 minutes, or until heated through. Top with remaining cheese and bake for another 10 minutes, or until cheese is melted. Serves 4.

225

Chad Rutan
Gooseberry Patch
I love this authentic taste of an Italian restaurant right from my oven!

Cheesy Shrimp Casserole

8-oz. pkg. wide egg noodles,
   uncooked
2 4-1/4 oz. cans tiny shrimp,
   drained
10-3/4 oz. can cream of shrimp
   or cream of celery soup
3/4 c. milk
1/2 c. mayonnaise
1/4 c. celery, diced
1 t. salt
1 T. green onion, chopped
1/2 c. shredded Cheddar cheese
1/4 c. chow mein noodles

Cook egg noodles according to
package directions; drain. Combine
with remaining ingredients except
chow mein noodles in an ungreased
11"x7" baking pan. Bake, uncovered,
at 350 degrees for 25 minutes. Top
with chow mein noodles and bake
for an additional 10 minutes.
Serves 4 to 6.

Jen Burnham
Delaware, OH

This is such an easy
recipe...everything is
mixed right in the
baking pan.

Potato Puff Casserole

1 lb. ground beef
10-3/4 oz. can cream of
    mushroom soup
3 14-1/2 oz. cans green beans,
    drained
12 slices pasteurized process
    cheese spread
16-oz. pkg. frozen potato puffs

In a skillet over medium heat,
brown beef; drain and stir in soup.
Pour beef mixture into a greased
13"x9" baking pan. Top with green
beans and sliced cheese. Arrange a
single layer of potato puffs over
cheese. Cover with aluminum
foil and bake at 400 degrees for
20 minutes, or until cheese is
melted. Uncover and bake again for
10 minutes, or until potato puffs are
golden. Serves 6 to 8.

227

**Dawn Henning
Gooseberry Patch**

A family-favorite recipe
that can be made in
advance and frozen for
a future hearty meal.

Blue-Ribbon Corn Dog Bake

1/3 c. sugar
1 egg, beaten
1 c. all-purpose flour
3/4 T. baking powder
1/2 t. salt
1/2 c. yellow cornmeal
1/2 T. butter, melted
3/4 c. milk
16-oz. pkg. hot dogs, sliced into
   bite-size pieces

In a small bowl, mix together sugar and egg. In a separate bowl, mix together flour, baking powder and salt. Add flour mixture to sugar mixture. Add cornmeal, butter and milk, stirring just to combine. Fold in hot dog pieces. Pour into a well-greased 8"x8" baking pan. Bake, uncovered, at 375 degrees for about 15 minutes, or until a toothpick inserted near the center comes out clean. Serves 6.

Tiffani Schulte
Wyandotte, MI
This casserole is oh-so easy and it really does taste like a county fair corn dog!

Oodles of Noodles Chili Bake

12-oz. pkg. wide egg noodles,
   uncooked
1 lb. ground beef
14-1/2 oz. can diced tomatoes
15-oz. can corn, drained
15-oz. can chili
1 c. shredded Cheddar cheese,
   divided

Cook noodles according to package
directions; drain and set aside.
Meanwhile, brown beef in a skillet
over medium heat; drain. Combine
tomatoes with juice and remaining
ingredients except 1/4 cup cheese in
a lightly greased 13"x9" baking pan.
Top with remaining cheese. Bake,
uncovered, at 350 degrees for about
20 minutes, or until heated through.
Serves 4.

Robin Kessler
Fresno, CA

Create a different dish
by adding your favorite
vegetables. It's foolproof
and delicious either way!

Sloppy Joe Casserole

1 lb. ground beef
1 onion, diced
1 green pepper, diced
salt to taste
10-3/4 oz. can tomato soup
1/2 c. water
1 t. Worcestershire sauce
7-1/2 oz. tube refrigerated
   biscuits
1/2 c. shredded Cheddar cheese

Brown beef with onion, pepper and salt in a skillet over medium heat; drain. Stir in soup, water and Worcestershire sauce; heat to a boil. Spoon beef mixture into a greased 1-1/2 quart casserole dish. Arrange biscuits on top of beef mixture around the edges of the dish. Bake, uncovered, at 400 degrees for 15 minutes, or until biscuits are golden. Sprinkle cheese over biscuits; bake again for 15 minutes, or until cheese is melted. Serves 4.

Amy Hunt
Traphill, NC

This is a less messy way
to eat a Sloppy Joe,
but just as good.

Cowpoke Casserole

1 lb. ground beef
1/2 onion, chopped
salt and pepper to taste
1 t. chili powder
15-1/2 oz. can chili beans
8-oz. can tomato sauce
1/2 c. water
8-1/2 oz. pkg. cornbread mix
1/3 c. milk
1 egg, beaten

Brown beef with onion in an oven-proof skillet over medium heat. Drain; add salt and pepper to taste. Stir in chili powder, beans, tomato sauce and water. Simmer for 5 minutes; remove from heat. In a separate bowl, stir together cornbread mix, milk and egg; spoon over beef mixture and place skillet in oven. Bake, uncovered, at 350 degrees for 25 minutes, or until cornbread topping is golden and cooked through. Serves 4 to 6.

231

Debbie Hutchinson
Spring, TX

A cast-iron skillet is perfect for this dish... it can go right into the oven to bake!

Reuben Casserole

6 slices rye bread, cubed
16-oz. can sauerkraut, drained
   and rinsed
1 lb. sliced deli corned beef,
   cut into strips
3/4 c. Thousand Island salad
   dressing
2 c. shredded Swiss cheese

Arrange bread cubes in a greased
13"x9" baking pan; cover with
sauerkraut. Layer corned beef over
sauerkraut; drizzle salad dressing over
top. Cover with aluminum foil and
bake at 400 degrees for 20 minutes.
Remove foil; sprinkle with cheese
and bake, uncovered, for another
10 minutes, or until cheese is melted
and bubbly. Serves 6.

Jo Ann

An all-time favorite deli
sandwich turned into a quick
and simple casserole!

Mom's Texas Hash

1 lb. ground beef
2 onions, sliced
1 green pepper, chopped
1 c. stewed tomatoes
1/2 to 1 t. chili powder
1 t. salt

Brown beef, onions and green pepper in a skillet over medium heat; drain. Stir in tomatoes with juice and seasonings. Cook over medium heat until warmed through, about 8 minutes; spoon into an ungreased one-quart casserole dish. Bake, uncovered, at 350 degrees for 15 to 20 minutes. Serves 4.

233

Ginger O'Connell
Hazel Park, MI

Simply said...this is good!

Autumn Pork Chop Bake

14-1/2 oz. can cream of celery
   soup
1-1/2 c. herb-flavored stuffing
   mix
1/2 c. corn
1/4 c. celery, chopped
4 boneless pork chops
1 t. brown sugar, packed
1 t. spicy brown mustard

In a bowl, combine soup, stuffing
mix, corn and celery. Spoon into a
greased 9" pie plate. Top with pork
chops. In a bowl, mix together
brown sugar and mustard; spoon
over pork chops. Bake, uncovered, at
400 degrees for 30 minutes, or until
hot and pork chops are cooked
through. Serves 4.

Elizabeth Gilvin
Lexington, KY
This is one of my family's
favorite recipes on
a cold day!

Company Breakfast Casserole

1/2 lb. bacon
1/2 c. onion, chopped
1 doz. eggs, beaten
1 c. milk
16-oz. pkg. frozen shredded
   hashbrowns, thawed
1-1/2 c. shredded sharp Cheddar
   cheese
1 t. salt
1/2 t. pepper

In a skillet over medium heat, cook
bacon until crisp. Crumble and set
aside, reserving 2 tablespoons
drippings. Sauté onion in reserved
drippings until tender; set aside. In
a bowl, beat eggs and milk; stir in
onion, bacon and remaining
ingredients. Pour into a greased
13"x9" baking pan. Bake, uncovered,
at 350 degrees for 40 to 45 minutes,
until a knife inserted near the middle
comes out clean. Serves 6.

235

**Vickie Tiche
Lincoln, CA**

This hearty breakfast
casserole is perfect
to serve to overnight
guests anytime.

Baked Stuffed Tomatoes

4 tomatoes
1/2 c. dry bread crumbs
2 t. butter, melted
1 t. grated Parmesan cheese
1/2 t. dried basil
1/2 t. dried oregano
2 t. fresh parsley, finely chopped
salt and pepper to taste

Slice tops off tomatoes; set aside.
Scoop out some of the pulp from
tomatoes; discard. Blend together
remaining ingredients. Spoon crumb
mixture evenly into each tomato,
pressing firmly. Place tomatoes in
a greased 9"x9" baking pan. Bake,
uncovered, at 350 degrees for
20 minutes, or until topping is
golden. Makes 4 servings.

Donna Dye
London, OH

Rediscover this old-fashioned
favorite...it's as good
as ever!

Mexican Lasagna

1 lb. ground beef
1-1/4 oz. pkg. taco seasoning
8-oz. pkg. 10-inch flour tortillas
8-oz. pkg. cream cheese,
   softened and divided
1 c. shredded Cheddar cheese,
   divided
8-oz. can tomato sauce, divided

Brown beef in a skillet over medium heat; drain. Add taco seasoning and cook according to package directions. Spread 2 tortillas with 1/4 of the cream cheese and place cheese-side up in an ungreased 13"x9" baking pan; spoon 1/4 of the beef mixture over tortillas. Top with 1/4 the shredded cheese and 1/4 the tomato sauce. Repeat layers 3 more times, ending with cheese. Bake, uncovered, at 350 degrees for about 25 minutes, or until heated through and cheese is melted. Serves 4 to 6.

237

Amanda Melancon
Hahira, GA

My daughter and I love this...plus we always have all the ingredients on hand!

Cheeseburger Bake

8-oz. tube refrigerated crescent
   rolls
1 lb. ground beef
1-1/4 oz. pkg. taco seasoning
15-oz. can tomato sauce
2 c. shredded Cheddar cheese

Unroll crescent roll dough; press
into a greased 9" round baking pan,
pinching seams closed. Bake at
350 degrees for 10 minutes; set aside.
Meanwhile, brown beef in a skillet
over medium heat; drain. Add taco
seasoning and sauce; heat through.
Spoon over crescent rolls and
sprinkle cheese on top. Bake,
uncovered, for 10 to 15 minutes.
Let stand 5 minutes before serving.
Serves 4.

Jennifer Williams
Los Angeles, CA
This hearty meal is great
after a long day of work
and errands...so filling.

Crescent Roll Lasagna

1-1/2 lbs. ground beef
1 onion, diced
salt and pepper to taste
15-oz. can tomato sauce
1 T. Worcestershire sauce
1/2 t. garlic salt
1 t. Italian seasoning, divided
2 T. brown sugar, packed
2 c. shredded Cheddar cheese
2 c. shredded mozzarella cheese
2 8-oz. tubes refrigerated
    crescent rolls
8-oz. container sour cream

239

In a skillet over medium heat, brown beef, onion, salt and pepper; drain. Add sauces, garlic salt, 1/2 teaspoon Italian seasoning and brown sugar. Transfer to a greased 13"x9" baking pan. Top with cheeses. Unroll crescent rolls; spread with about a tablespoon of sour cream and sprinkle with remaining Italian seasoning. Roll up crescent rolls; place on top of cheese. Bake, uncovered, at 350 degrees for 35 to 40 minutes, until bubbly and rolls are golden. Serves 6 to 8.

Faith Bedard
Hallock, MN

A family favorite...it's
so good!

Eggplant Casserole

1 lb. ground beef
1 onion, diced
salt, pepper and garlic powder
    to taste
1 eggplant, quartered
2 eggs, beaten
2 T. grated Parmesan cheese
10 saltine crackers, crushed
2 T. butter, sliced

Brown beef and onion with salt, pepper and garlic powder in a skillet over medium heat; drain. Meanwhile, in a saucepan, cover eggplant with water; boil until tender. Scoop cooked eggplant out of its skin; let cool. Discard skin. Combine beef mixture, eggplant, eggs and Parmesan in a greased 13"x9" baking pan, mixing well. Top with crackers and dot with butter. Bake, uncovered, at 325 degrees for 30 minutes, or until heated through. Serves 6 to 8.

Gina Robinson
Streetman, TX

This recipe was a favorite when I was growing up. It has been passed on for generations.

Mexican Cornbread Bake

Terri Taylor
Jonesville, LA

Spicy beef tucked
between layers of golden
cornbread...yum!

1 lb. ground beef
4-1/2 oz. can chopped green
   chiles
1 onion, chopped
2 t. Mexican seasoning
1 T. chili powder
8-oz. can Mexican-style tomato
   sauce
8-1/2 oz. pkg. cornbread mix

Brown beef in a skillet over medium heat; drain. Add chiles, onion and seasonings; cook until onion is tender. Add tomato sauce and simmer. Prepare cornbread mix according to package directions; pour half the batter into a greased 2-quart casserole dish. Spoon beef mixture over batter; top with remaining batter. Bake, uncovered, at 350 degrees for 25 to 30 minutes, until golden. Serves 4 to 6.

241

Brock's Pimento & Cheese Grits Casserole

3 c. quick-cooking grits, uncooked
1/2 c. butter
1/2 c. whipping cream
1 t. salt
16-oz. pkg. shredded Cheddar cheese
4-oz. jar diced pimentos, drained
1 c. mayonnaise
8-oz. pkg. cream cheese, softened
2 t. pepper
1/2 c. green onions, chopped

Cook grits according to package directions. In a bowl, combine grits, butter, cream and salt. In a separate bowl, combine remaining ingredients except onions; mix well. Combine the 2 mixtures; stir together. Pour into a greased 13"x9" baking pan. Bake, uncovered, at 375 degrees for 35 to 40 minutes, until bubbly. Top with onions. Serves 8.

Brock Rogers
Louisville, MS
This is a different spin on traditional Southern cheese grits.

Harvest Casserole

1/2 c. long-cooking rice,
  uncooked
4 redskin potatoes, cut into
  thin wedges
1/4 c. butter, sliced and divided
1 T. fresh sage, chopped
3 red peppers, chopped
1 onion, sliced
2 zucchini, thinly sliced
1 c. shredded Cheddar cheese

Cook rice according to package directions; set aside. Place potatoes in a greased 2-1/2 quart casserole dish. Dot with half the butter; layer half the sage, peppers, onion, zucchini and rice. Layer ingredients again; cover with aluminum foil. Bake at 350 degrees for one hour, or until potatoes are tender. Remove foil; sprinkle cheese over top and return to oven until cheese is melted. Serves 6.

243

Regina Wickline
Pebble Beach, CA

This casserole is packed full of wonderful vegetables grown in your own backyard or from the nearest farmers' market.

Hearty Stuffed Pepper Casserole

2-1/2 c. herb-flavored stuffing
 mix, divided
1 T. butter, melted
1 lb. ground beef
1/2 c. onion, chopped
14-1/2 oz. can whole tomatoes,
 chopped
8-oz. can corn, drained
salt and pepper to taste
2 green peppers, quartered

Mix together 1/4 cup dry stuffing
mix and butter; set aside. Brown
beef and onion in a skillet over
medium-high heat; drain. Stir in
tomatoes, corn, salt and pepper;
add remaining stuffing mix. Arrange
green peppers in an ungreased
2-quart casserole dish; spoon beef
mixture over top. Cover and bake
at 400 degrees for 25 minutes.
Sprinkle with reserved stuffing
mixture. Bake, uncovered, for
5 additional minutes, or until
peppers are tender. Serves 4 to 6.

Vickie

Love stuffed peppers? Try
this casserole version for
a new family favorite!

Taco-Filled Pasta Shells

2 lbs. ground beef
2 1-1/4 oz. pkgs. taco seasoning
8-oz. pkg. cream cheese, cubed
2 12-oz. pkgs. jumbo pasta
    shells, uncooked
1/4 c. butter, melted
1 c. salsa
1 c. taco sauce
1 c. shredded Cheddar cheese
1 c. shredded Monterey Jack
    cheese
1-1/2 c. tortilla chips, crushed
Optional: sour cream, chopped
    green onions

245

Brown beef in a skillet over medium heat; drain. Add taco seasoning and cook according to package directions. Add cream cheese; stir to melt. Remove beef mixture to a bowl and chill for one hour. Meanwhile, cook pasta shells according to package directions; drain. Toss shells with butter. Fill each shell with 3 tablespoons of beef mixture. Spoon salsa into a greased 13"x9" baking pan; place shells on top of salsa and cover with taco sauce. Bake, covered, at 350 degrees for 30 minutes. Uncover, sprinkle with cheeses and tortilla chips. Bake for 15 minutes, or until heated through. Serves 4 to 6.

Brittany Cornelius
Chambersburg, PA

A Mexican twist on an Italian dish...my whole family loves this!

Maggie's Kickin' King Ranch Chicken

Maggie Jo Tucker
Hartsfield, GA
I got this recipe from my dear friend Aunt B, but I have adapted it to fit our tastes!

5 to 6 boneless, skinless chicken
  breasts, cooked and cubed
2 10-3/4 oz. cans cream of
  chicken soup
2 10-3/4 oz. cans cream of
  mushroom soup
2 10-oz. cans diced tomatoes
  with green chiles
1 T. chili powder
2 t. garlic salt
1-1/3 c. water
salt and pepper to taste
2 18-oz. pkgs. restaurant-style
  tortilla chips, divided
2 12-oz. pkgs. shredded
  Cheddar cheese

In a large bowl, combine chicken and remaining ingredients except chips and cheese; mix well. Place chips in a single layer in the bottom and up the sides of an ungreased 15"x10" baking pan; reserve any remaining chips. Spoon chicken mixture over chips. Cover with cheese. Bake, uncovered, at 350 degrees for 30 minutes, or until bubbly. Serve with remaining chips. Serves 8 to 10.

Chicken-Broccoli Divan

2 c. cooked chicken, cubed
16-oz. pkg. frozen broccoli
    flowerets, thawed
2 10-3/4 oz. cans cream of
    chicken soup
3/4 c. mayonnaise
1 t. lemon juice
1/2 c. shredded Cheddar cheese

Place chicken in a greased
13"x9" baking pan. Layer broccoli
on top. In a bowl, stir together soup,
mayonnaise and lemon juice. Pour
soup mixture over broccoli; top
with cheese. Bake, uncovered, at
350 degrees for 45 minutes, or
until bubbly. Serves 4.

247

Tiffany Mayberry
Harriman, TN

This is a delightful recipe
I remember my mother
cooking for me when
I was a little girl.

Green Bean, Ham & Potato Bake

1 onion, chopped
2 cloves garlic, minced
1 T. butter
3 potatoes, diced
salt and pepper to taste
2 14-1/2 oz. cans green beans,
   drained
1-1/2 c. cooked ham, cubed
2 sprigs fresh rosemary, chopped
1 c. water

In a skillet over medium-high heat, sauté onion and garlic in butter; add potatoes, salt and pepper. Cook until potatoes are crisp. In a greased 13"x9" baking pan, combine potato mixture, green beans, ham and rosemary. Drizzle water over all. Cover with aluminum foil and bake at 350 degrees for one hour, or until potatoes are tender. Serves 6.

Rachel Kowasic
Connellsville, PA
I grew up watching my stepmom make this tasty recipe with fresh green beans from her garden.

Easy Cheesy Ratatouille

1 eggplant, peeled and cut into
   1-inch cubes
1 onion, diced
1 red pepper, diced
1 zucchini, cut into 1-inch cubes
1/4 c. sun-dried tomato
   vinaigrette
14-1/2 oz. can diced tomatoes
1/4 c. grated Parmesan cheese
1 c. shredded mozzarella cheese

Sauté vegetables with vinaigrette
in a large oven-safe skillet over
medium heat. Add tomatoes with
juice; cook for 15 minutes. Sprinkle
with cheeses. Bake, uncovered, at
350 degrees for 15 minutes, or until
vegetables are tender. Serves 6 to 8.

249

Amy Butcher
Columbus, GA
When I first had this at a
church potluck, I made sure
to go back for seconds and
to ask for the recipe!

Johnny Marzetti

2 T. oil
1 onion, chopped
1 green pepper, chopped
1 lb. ground beef
28-oz. jar spaghetti sauce
1-1/2 c. elbow macaroni, cooked
2 c. shredded Cheddar cheese

Heat oil in a skillet. Add onion and green pepper; sauté until softened. Add beef and cook until browned; drain. Stir in spaghetti sauce and macaroni; pour into an ungreased 13"x9" baking pan. Sprinkle with cheese. Bake, uncovered, at 350 degrees for one hour. Serves 4 to 6.

Linda Karner
Pisgah Forest, NC

No one knows about this dish's mysterious name...but everyone agrees it tastes incredible!

Zucchini Boats

1 lb. ground beef
1 onion, chopped
16-oz. jar spaghetti sauce
2 large zucchini, halved
    lengthwise
salt and pepper to taste
1/2 c. grated parmesan cheese
1 c. shredded mozzarella cheese

Brown beef and onion in a skillet over medium heat; drain. Add spaghetti sauce to beef mixture and stir until combined. Meanwhile, lay zucchini halves, cut-side down, on a microwave-safe plate. Cook on high setting until fork-tender, about 5 to 10 minutes. Scoop out seeds and some surrounding pulp; discard. Sprinkle zucchini halves with salt and pepper; place in a greased 13"x9" baking pan. Spoon beef mixture into hollowed-out zucchini halves and top with cheeses. Bake, uncovered, at 350 degrees for about 40 minutes, or until heated through and cheese is bubbly. Serves 4.

251

Audrey Piatti
Leonardo, NJ

I came up with this recipe because I could never decide what to do with all my zucchini...who knew these would be so good?

Buffalo Chicken Quinoa Casserole

1 c. quinoa, uncooked
3 c. shredded Cheddar cheese,
    divided
1 c. buffalo wing sauce, divided
1 c. sour cream
1/4 c. butter, softened
1/4 c. milk
1/2 t. garlic salt
1/4 t. pepper
1 t. dried basil
4 boneless, skinless chicken
    breasts, cooked and cubed

Cook quinoa according to package
directions. Meanwhile, in a large
bowl, combine 2 cups cheese and
1/2 cup buffalo wing sauce with
remaining ingredients except chicken
and quinoa. Fold in quinoa. Spread
mixture into a greased 13"x9" baking
pan. Top with chicken. Drizzle with
remaining buffalo wing sauce and
sprinkle with remaining cheese.
Bake, covered, at 350 degrees for
45 minutes, or until heated through
and bubbly. Serves 8.

Trish McGregor
Prospect, VA

Forged out of my
family's love of buffalo
chicken...this casserole
has become a favorite!

Cheesy Baked Tortellini

10-oz. pkg. refrigerated cheese
   tortellini
2 c. marinara sauce
1/3 c. mascarpone cheese or
   softened cream cheese
1/4 c. fresh Italian parsley,
   chopped
2 t. fresh thyme, chopped
5 slices smoked mozzarella cheese
1/4 c. shredded Parmesan cheese

Prepare tortellini according to
package directions; drain and set
aside. Meanwhile, in a bowl,
combine marinara sauce, mascarpone
or cream cheese, parsley and thyme.
Fold in tortellini. Transfer to a
greased 9"x9" baking pan. Top with
mozzarella and Parmesan cheeses.
Bake, covered, at 350 degrees for
about 30 minutes, or until cheese
is melted and sauce is bubbly.
Serves 4 to 6.

253

Pat Wissler
Harrisburg, PA

When I make this hearty dish,
I usually double the recipe
and freeze some for later...
very convenient!

Cheesy Sausage-Potato Casserole

3 to 4 potatoes, sliced
1 lb. smoked sausage, sliced
1 onion, chopped
1/2 c. butter, sliced
1 c. shredded Cheddar cheese

Layer potatoes, sausage and onion in a 13"x9" baking pan sprayed with non-stick vegetable spray. Dot with butter; sprinkle with cheese. Bake, uncovered, at 350 degrees for 1-1/2 hours, or until potatoes are tender. Serves 6 to 8.

J.J. Presley
Portland, TX
Add some fresh green beans too if you like.

Crab & Shrimp Casserole

2 8-oz. cans crabmeat, drained
2 4-oz. cans tiny shrimp,
    drained
2 c. celery, chopped
1 green pepper, chopped
1 onion, chopped
1 T. Worcestershire sauce
1 t. sugar
1 c. mayonnaise
salt and pepper to taste
1 c. soft bread crumbs, buttered
2 T. lemon juice
Garnish: thin lemon slices

255

Mix together all ingredients except
bread crumbs, lemon juice and
garnish. Place in a greased
13"x9" baking pan. Spread bread
crumbs over crab mixture. Bake,
uncovered, at 350 degrees for
30 to 45 minutes, until heated
through. Sprinkle lemon juice over
casserole. Garnish with lemon slices.
Serves 4 to 6.

Jennie Gist
Gooseberry Patch

The yummy taste of
the sea in a
convenient casserole!

Beef Burgundy

1-1/2 lb. beef sirloin, cubed
2 1-1/2 oz. pkgs. onion soup mix
2 10-3/4 oz. cans cream of
   mushroom soup
1/2 c. burgundy wine or beef
   broth
1/2 c. water
cooked rice or egg noodles

Combine all ingredients except rice or noodles in a Dutch oven. Bake, covered, at 325 degrees for 2-1/2 hours, or until bubbly and beef is cooked through. Serve beef mixture over rice or noodles. Makes 6 to 8 servings.

Melia Himich
Manchester, MI

An easy-to-prepare dish that's delicious served over noodles or rice.

Meatball Sub Casserole

1 loaf Italian bread, cut into
   1-inch thick slices
8-oz. pkg. cream cheese,
   softened
1/2 c. mayonnaise
1 t. Italian seasoning
1/4 t. pepper
2 c. shredded mozzarella cheese,
   divided
1-lb. pkg. frozen meatballs,
   thawed
28-oz. jar pasta sauce
1 c. water

Arrange bread slices in a single layer
in an ungreased 13"x9" baking pan;
set aside. In a bowl, combine cream
cheese, mayonnaise and seasonings;
spread over bread slices. Sprinkle
with 1/2 cup cheese; set aside. Gently
mix together meatballs, spaghetti
sauce and water; spoon over cheese.
Sprinkle with remaining cheese.
Bake, uncovered, at 350 degrees for
30 minutes. Serves 4.

257

Christi Wroe
Bedford, PA

Serve this tasty casserole
with a green salad and
garlic bread...delicious!

Eggplant Parmesan

Tammy Dillow
Raceland, KY

For me, this is a down-home
dish that's great to enjoy
with family & friends, no
matter what the occasion.

4 eggs, beaten
3 T. water
2 eggplants, peeled and sliced
    1/4-inch thick
2 c. Italian-style dry bread
    crumbs
1-1/2 c. grated Parmesan cheese,
    divided
28-oz. jar garden-style pasta
    sauce, divided
1-1/2 c. shredded mozzarella
    cheese

Whisk together eggs and water in a
shallow bowl. Dip eggplant slices into
egg mixture. Arrange slices in a single
layer on a greased baking sheet; bake
at 350 degrees for 25 minutes, or
until tender. Set aside. Mix bread
crumbs and 1/2 cup Parmesan cheese;
set aside. Spread a small amount of
sauce in an ungreased 13"x9" baking
pan; layer half the eggplant, one cup
sauce and one cup crumb mixture.
Repeat layering. Cover with
aluminum foil and bake for
45 minutes. Remove foil; sprinkle
with mozzarella cheese. Bake,
uncovered, for an additional
10 minutes. Serves 6 to 8.

Sausage & Chicken Cassoulet

1 lb. hot Italian ground pork
   sausage
1 c. carrot, peeled and thinly
   sliced
1 onion, diced
2 t. garlic, minced
1 c. red wine or beef broth
2 T. tomato paste
1 bay leaf
1 t. dried thyme
1 t. dried rosemary
salt and pepper to taste
2 c. cooked chicken, diced
2 15-oz. cans Great Northern
   beans

259

Brown sausage in an oven-safe Dutch
oven over medium heat; drain. Add
carrot, onion and garlic. Sauté for
3 minutes. Add wine or broth,
tomato paste and seasonings; bring
to a boil. Remove from heat; stir in
chicken and beans with liquid. Bake,
covered, at 350 degrees for
45 minutes, or until bubbly. Discard
bay leaf before serving. Serves 4 to 6.

Diane Stout
Zeeland, MI

This savory casserole is
full of wonderful flavors...
better bring along some
recipe cards to share!

Polenta Casserole

3 c. water
1 t. salt
1 c. yellow cornmeal
1/2 t. Montreal steak seasoning
1 c. shredded sharp Cheddar
   cheese, divided
1 lb. ground beef
1 c. onion, chopped
1 zucchini, halved lengthwise and
   sliced
1 T. olive oil
2 14-1/2 oz. cans diced tomatoes,
   drained
6-oz. can tomato paste
Garnish: fresh parsley, chopped

In a 2-quart saucepan, bring water and salt to a boil. Whisk in cornmeal; reduce heat to low. Simmer, whisking constantly, for 3 minutes, or until thickened. Remove from heat; stir in steak seasoning and 1/4 cup cheese. Spread cornmeal mixture into a greased 11"x7" baking pan. Brown beef with onion and zucchini in oil in a skillet over medium-high heat; drain. Stir in tomatoes and tomato paste; simmer for 10 minutes, stirring often. Spoon beef mixture over cornmeal mixture; sprinkle with remaining cheese. Bake, uncovered, at 350 degrees for 30 minutes, or until bubbly. Garnish with parsley. Serves 6.

Gail Blain Prather
Hastings, NE
Easy, filling and
best of all, yummy!

Mom's Chicken Casserole

6-oz. pkg. rice pilaf mix
4 to 6 boneless, skinless chicken
   breasts
2 c. stewed tomatoes

Prepare rice pilaf according to package directions, cooking for just half the time. Transfer pilaf to a greased 13"x9" baking pan. Place chicken breasts over pilaf. Spoon tomatoes over chicken. Bake, covered with aluminum foil, at 350 degrees for one hour, or until chicken juices run clear and all liquid is absorbed. Serves 4 to 6.

261

Samantha Fishkin
Lauderdale Lakes, FL

This meal is very easy to create, uses very few ingredients and is delicious!

Daddy's Shepherd's Pie

1 lb. ground beef
10-3/4 oz. can cream of
   mushroom soup
2/3 c. water
7.2-oz. pkg. homestyle creamy
   butter-flavored instant mashed
   potato flakes
2 c. corn
8-oz. pkg. shredded Cheddar
   cheese

Brown beef in a skillet over medium heat; drain. Stir in soup and water; simmer until heated through. Meanwhile, prepare potato flakes as package directs; set aside. Place beef mixture in a 13"x9" baking pan sprayed with non-stick vegetable spray. Top with corn; spread potatoes evenly across top. Sprinkle with cheese. Bake, uncovered, at 425 degrees for about 10 minutes, or until hot and cheese is melted. Makes 6 to 8 servings.

Sheila Wakeman
Winnsboro, TX

I can remember going to Dad's house on the weekends, and we would make this dish together.

Hobo Dinner

1-1/2 lbs. ground beef
1 t. Worcestershire sauce
1/2 t. seasoned pepper
1/8 t. garlic powder
3 redskin potatoes, sliced
1 onion, sliced
3 carrots, peeled and sliced
olive oil and dried parsley
   to taste

In a bowl, combine beef, Worcestershire sauce, pepper and garlic powder; form into 4 to 6 patties. Place each patty on an 18-inch length of aluminum foil. Divide slices of potato, onion and carrots evenly and place on top of each patty. Sprinkle with olive oil and parsley to taste. Wrap tightly in aluminum foil and arrange packets on a baking sheet. Bake at 375 degrees for one hour, or until vegetables are tender and beef is cooked through. Serves 4 to 6.

263

Denise Piccirilli
Huber Heights, OH

My mom and I have made this recipe for years. It's quick, delicious and so easy the kids can help assemble it.

Baked Chicken Chow Mein

10-3/4 oz. can cream of chicken
  soup
10-3/4 oz. can cream of celery
  soup
5-oz. can evaporated milk
4-oz. can mushroom stems and
  pieces, drained
8-oz. can water chestnuts,
  drained and chopped
2 c. cooked chicken, cubed
5-oz. can chow mein noodles,
  divided
2 t. Worcestershire sauce
1 to 2 t. curry powder
2 T. butter

In a bowl, combine soups and milk;
fold in mushrooms, water chestnuts,
chicken and half the chow mein
noodles. Sprinkle with Worcestershire
sauce and curry powder; stir to
combine. Spread into a greased
2-quart casserole dish. Top with
remaining noodles; dot with butter.
Bake, uncovered, at 350 degrees
for 30 minutes, or until bubbly.
Serves 4 to 6.

Judi Leaming
Dover, DE
Our daughter, Ami, earned
a 4-H Blue Ribbon for
this dish!

Hunter's Pie

1 lb. roast beef, cooked and
  cubed
12-oz. jar beef gravy
8-oz. can sliced carrots, drained
8-oz. can green beans, drained
9-inch deep-dish pie crust,
  baked
11-oz. tube refrigerated bread
  sticks

Combine all ingredients except pie
crust and bread sticks; spread into
pie crust. Arrange unbaked bread
sticks on top, criss-cross style. Bake
at 350 degrees for 20 minutes, or
until heated through and bread sticks
are golden. Serves 4.

265

Heidi Maurer
Garrett, IN

My 3-year-old son Hunter
loves this and my 8-year-old
son Luke does too...but
without the beans!

Shipwreck Casserole

1 lb. lean ground beef
1/4 t. salt
1/4 t. pepper
4 potatoes, peeled and sliced
1 onion, chopped
8-oz. can pork & beans
10-3/4 oz. can tomato soup

In a skillet over medium heat, brown beef with salt and pepper; drain and set aside. Place potatoes in a greased 2-quart casserole dish; top with onion. Cover with beef mixture. Spoon pork & beans over beef, then pour tomato soup over all. Bake, covered, at 375 degrees for one hour, or until potatoes are tender and casserole is bubbly. Serves 6 to 8.

Janis Parr
Campbellford, Ontario
The kids come running to the table whenever I make Shipwreck Casserole!

Ham & Cheese Spaghetti

1 lb. cooked ham, cubed
1 to 2 t. olive oil
1 green pepper, diced
1 onion, diced
2 to 3 cloves garlic, pressed
15-oz. can tomato sauce
14-1/2 oz. can diced tomatoes
Italian seasoning to taste
16-oz. pkg. spaghetti, uncooked
16-oz. pkg. sliced American
    cheese

267

In a skillet over medium heat, lightly brown ham in oil. Add pepper and onion; sauté until tender. Stir in garlic, tomato sauce, tomatoes with juice and seasoning; bring to a boil. Reduce heat; cover and simmer for 20 to 30 minutes, stirring occasionally. Meanwhile, cook spaghetti according to package directions; drain. In a greased 13"x9" baking pan, place a layer of spaghetti, a layer of ham mixture and 3 to 4 cheese slices. Repeat layering 2 to 3 times, ending with sauce and cheese. Bake, uncovered, at 375 degrees for about 10 minutes, or until hot and bubbly. Serves 4 to 6.

Cynthia Besse
Midlothian, TX

This family favorite dates back to the Depression and has been a regular at our family table ever since.

Sweet Corn & Rice Casserole

2 T. butter
1 green pepper, chopped
1 onion, chopped
15-1/2 oz. can creamed corn
11-oz. can sweet corn & diced
　peppers, drained
11-oz. can corn, drained
6 c. cooked rice
10-oz. can diced tomatoes with
　green chiles, drained
8-oz. pkg. mild Mexican
　pasteurized process cheese
　spread, cubed
1/2 t. salt
1/4 t. pepper
1/2 c. shredded Cheddar cheese

Melt butter in a large skillet over
medium heat. Add green pepper and
onion; sauté 5 minutes, or until
tender. Stir in remaining ingredients
except shredded cheese; spoon into
a lightly greased 13"x9" baking pan.
Bake, uncovered, at 350 degrees for
25 to 30 minutes, until heated
through. Top with shredded cheese;
bake an additional 5 minutes, until
cheese melts. Makes 10 to 12 servings.

Linda Stone
Algood, TN

Roll up leftovers in
a flour tortilla for
a hearty snack.

Baked Chicken Jambalaya

1 lb. pkg. smoked beef sausage,
   sliced
1/4 c. butter
4 c. cooked chicken, cubed
16-oz. pkg. frozen mixed
   vegetables, thawed
1 onion, sliced
4 stalks celery, sliced
1 green pepper, thinly sliced
2 c. shredded mozzarella or
   Cheddar cheese
16-oz. pkg. bowtie pasta,
   cooked

269

In a skillet over medium-high heat,
sauté sausage in butter until
browned. Add chicken to skillet with
sausage. Transfer sausage mixture
into a 13"x9" baking pan; add mixed
vegetables, onion, celery and green
pepper. Top with cheese and cover
with aluminum foil. Bake at
350 degrees for about 30 minutes,
or until veggies are crisp-tender and
cheese is melted. Serve over pasta.
Serves 8.

Vicki Holland
Hampton, GA

I came up with this dish on
short notice to feed a bunch
of hungry teenagers with
what I had on hand. I was
surprised at the great
blend of flavors.

Hamburger Stroganoff Casserole

16-oz. pkg. wide egg noodles,
 uncooked
2 lbs. ground beef
1 onion, chopped
10-3/4 oz. can low-fat cream
 of mushroom soup
8-oz. container sour cream
salt and pepper to taste

Cook noodles according to package
directions; drain. Meanwhile,
brown beef and onion in a large
skillet over medium heat; drain.
Mix soup and sour cream into beef
mixture; add noodles. Season with
salt and pepper. Spoon into a lightly
greased 13"x9" baking pan. Bake,
uncovered, at 350 degrees for
30 minutes, or until heated through.
Serves 8 to 10.

Pamela Berry
Huntington, IN

This casserole is a
huge hit whenever I
put it on the table!

Apple-Pork Chop Casserole

1 T. oil
8 boneless pork chops
2 6-oz. pkgs. herb-flavored
   stuffing mix
2 21-oz. cans apple pie filling

Heat oil in a skillet over medium-high heat. Cook pork chops in oil until both sides are browned. Meanwhile, prepare stuffing according to package directions. Pour pie filling into a lightly greased 13"x9" baking pan; lay pork chops on top. Cover with stuffing. Bake, uncovered, at 325 degrees for 45 minutes to one hour, until pork chops are cooked through. Serves 8.

271

Gayla Reyes
Hamilton, OH

One of my family's favorites.
It's so quick and easy.

Chicken & Asparagus Bake

6 boneless, skinless chicken
  breasts, cooked and cubed
3 14-1/2 oz. cans asparagus
  pieces, drained
2-oz. jar chopped pimentos,
  drained
3/4 c. slivered almonds
3 10-3/4 oz. cans cream of
  mushroom soup
2 2.8-oz. cans French fried
  onions

Layer chicken, asparagus, pimentos,
almonds and soup in a lightly greased
2-1/2 quart casserole dish. Cover with
aluminum foil; bake at 350 degrees
for 30 to 40 minutes, until bubbly.
Uncover and top with onions. Bake
for an additional 5 minutes. Serves
6 to 8.

Marilyn Morel
Keene, NH

A delicious casserole that's
simple to prepare and bakes
in under 45 minutes!

Hearty Breakfast Casserole

6 to 8 bread slices
3-oz. pkg. ready-to-use bacon
    crumbles
1 lb. cooked ham, diced, or
    ground pork sausage, browned
2 c. shredded Cheddar cheese
10 eggs, beaten
1 c. milk
1 t. salt
1 t. pepper

Arrange bread slices in a single layer
in a greased 13"x9" baking pan; top
with bacon and ham or sausage.
Sprinkle with cheese. Whisk together
remaining ingredients. Pour egg
mixture over top. Cover with
aluminum foil and refrigerate
overnight. Bake, covered, at
350 degrees for 45 minutes to
one hour, until center is set.
Serves 12.

273

**Tracie Spencer
Rogers, KY**

An easy-to-assemble
make-ahead breakfast...
perfect for busy
mornings or when you
have brunch guests!

Broccoli Supreme

1 egg, beaten
10-oz. pkg. frozen chopped
  broccoli, partially thawed
  and drained
8-1/2 oz. can creamed corn
1 T. onion, grated
1/4 t. salt
1/8 t. pepper
1 c. herb-flavored stuffing mix
3 T. butter, melted

In a bowl, combine egg, broccoli,
corn, onion, salt and pepper. In a
separate bowl, toss stuffing mix
with butter. Stir 3/4 cup of stuffing
mixture into egg mixture. Turn into
an ungreased 8"x8" baking pan.
Sprinkle with remaining stuffing
mixture. Bake, uncovered, at
350 degrees for 35 to 40 minutes,
until bubbly. Makes 6 to 8 servings.

Linda Belon
Wintersville, OH
A delicious side that
whips up in a jiffy!

Family-Favorite Corn Soufflé

15-oz. can corn, drained
8-1/2 oz. pkg. cornbread mix
14-3/4 oz. can creamed corn
1 c. sour cream
1/4 c. butter, melted
8-oz. pkg. shredded Cheddar
  cheese

Combine all ingredients except
cheese. Pour into a lightly greased
13"x9" baking pan. Cover with
aluminum foil. Bake at 350 degrees
for 30 minutes. Uncover; top with
cheese. Return to oven and continue
baking until cheese is bubbly and
golden, about 15 minutes.
Serves 8 to 10.

275

Donna Maltman
Toledo, OH

An absolute must-have for
Thanksgiving dinner.

Italian Pie

1 lb. ground beef
garlic salt and pepper to taste
16-oz. jar spaghetti sauce
2 8-oz. cans refrigerated
   crescent rolls
1/2 c. shredded mozzarella cheese
1/2 c. shredded Colby cheese

Season beef with garlic salt and
pepper to taste; brown in a skillet
over medium heat. Drain; add
spaghetti sauce to beef and simmer
for 5 minutes. Layer one can of
crescent rolls in the bottom of a
greased 13"x9" baking dish; spread
rolls to edges of pan. Spoon beef
mixture over rolls; layer cheeses
on top. Spread remaining can of
crescent rolls over cheese layer;
cover with aluminum foil. Bake at
350 degrees for 30 minutes. Remove
foil and bake 15 more minutes, or
until golden. Makes 12 servings.

Becky Hawkins
Spearfish, SD

Serve with a crisp Caesar
salad for a complete meal.

Curry Chicken Casserole

1 c. long-cooking rice, uncooked
14-1/2 oz. can French-cut green
    beans, drained and divided
3 c. cooked chicken, chopped
8-oz. can sliced water chestnuts,
    drained
10-3/4 oz. can cream of chicken
    soup
1/4 c. chicken broth
1 c. mayonnaise
1 t. curry powder
1 c. French fried onions

Cook rice according to package
directions. Combine rice, half the
beans and remaining ingredients
except onions in a greased
13"x9" baking pan; mix well. Top
with remaining beans. Bake,
uncovered, at 350 degrees for
25 minutes, or until bubbling.
Sprinkle onions over top and bake
for another 5 minutes. Serves 6.

277

Jodi Griggs
Richmond, KY
My mother-in-law makes this
casserole for Sunday dinner,
and we all love it!

Seafood Enchiladas

Stephanie Monroe
Franklin, TN
These are great topped
with some thick and chunky
salsa plus a dollop
of sour cream!

3 c. chicken broth
1/3 c. all-purpose flour
14-1/2 oz. can diced tomatoes
3 green chiles, chopped
1/2 c. onion, chopped
1/2 t. garlic, minced
1 t. sugar
1 t. ground cumin
1/2 t. dried basil
1/2 t. dried oregano
salt and pepper to taste
1 lb. crabmeat
1/2 lb. cooked shrimp
12-oz. pkg. shredded Monterey
   Jack cheese
12 10-inch flour tortillas
3/4 c. sour cream

Combine broth with flour in a
saucepan. Cook over medium heat
until thickened, stirring constantly.
Add tomatoes with juice, chiles,
onion, garlic, sugar and seasonings.
Bring to a simmer, stirring frequently.
Remove from heat. Divide seafood
and half of cheese evenly among
tortillas; roll up and arrange seam-
side down in a greased 15"x10" baking
pan. Blend sour cream into tomato
mixture. Spoon tomato mixture over
enchiladas; sprinkle with remaining
cheese. Bake, uncovered, at
400 degrees for 15 minutes, or
until cheese melts. Serves 12.

Alabama Chicken Casserole

2 to 3 c. cooked chicken,
   chopped
4 eggs, hard-boiled, peeled
   and chopped
2 c. cooked rice
1-1/2 c. celery, chopped
1 onion, chopped
2 10-3/4 oz. cans cream of
   mushroom soup
1 c. mayonnaise
2 T. lemon juice
3-oz. pkg. slivered almonds
5-oz. can chow mein noodles

Mix all ingredients except noodles
in a large bowl. Transfer to a greased
13"x9" baking pan. Cover and
refrigerate overnight. Uncover and
bake at 350 degrees for one hour,
or until hot and bubbly. Top with
noodles; return to oven for
5 minutes. Makes 10 to 12 servings.

279

Betty Lou Wright
Hendersonville, TN

If I had a nickel for
every time this make-ahead
casserole has been carried
to a potluck, I'd be a
wealthy woman!

Parmesan Scalloped Potatoes

2 lbs. Yukon Gold potatoes,
   thinly sliced
3 c. whipping cream
1/4 c. fresh parsley, chopped
2 cloves garlic, chopped
1-1/2 t. salt
1/4 t. pepper
1/3 c. grated Parmesan cheese

Layer potatoes in a lightly greased
13"x9" baking pan. In a bowl, stir
together remaining ingredients
except cheese; pour over potatoes.
Bake, uncovered, at 400 degrees
for 30 minutes, stirring gently every
10 minutes. Sprinkle with cheese;
bake again for about 15 minutes, or
until bubbly and golden. Let stand
10 minutes before serving. Serves 8.

Tina Goodpasture
Meadowview, VA

Whether you eat them hot,
cold or warm...these are some
great scalloped potatoes!

Hearty Tortilla Casserole

2 lbs. ground beef
1 onion, chopped
2 t. instant coffee granules
1 t. salt
1 t. pepper
1 T. chili powder
29-oz. can tomato sauce, divided
12 10-inch flour tortillas
1/2 c. cream cheese, softened
1/3 c. water
2 c. shredded Cheddar or
    mozzarella cheese
12 black olives, sliced

281

Brown beef and onion in a skillet over medium heat; drain. Add coffee granules, seasonings and half the tomato sauce to beef mixture; set aside. Spread each tortilla with cream cheese. Add 1/4 cup of beef mixture to each tortilla and fold over. Place folded tortillas in a greased 13"x9" baking pan. Top with any remaining beef mixture. In a bowl, combine water and remaining tomato sauce; drizzle over tortillas. Sprinkle cheese and olives on top. Cover with aluminum foil and bake at 375 degrees for about 25 minutes, until heated through. Serves 6 to 8.

Angela Murphy
Tempe, AZ
A hint of coffee brings a warm heartiness to this dish!

Famous Calico Beans

1 lb. ground beef
1/4 lb. bacon, chopped
1 onion, chopped
16-oz. can pork & beans
15-oz. can kidney beans, drained
   and liquid reserved
15-oz. can butter beans, drained
   and liquid reserved
1/2 c. catsup
1/2 c. brown sugar, packed
2 T. vinegar
1/2 t. salt

Brown beef, bacon and onion in a
large skillet over medium heat; drain.
Spread beans in a lightly greased
13"x9" baking pan; add beef mixture.
In a bowl, combine remaining
ingredients; pour over beef mixture.
If more liquid is needed, add
reserved liquid from beans. Bake,
uncovered, at 350 degrees for
one hour. Serves 8.

Barbara Harman
Petersburg, WV
We always enjoy these beans
at our church get-togethers.
No matter who brings them,
they're always a hit.

Peg's Tomato-Bacon Pie

2 to 3 tomatoes, peeled
   and sliced
9-inch pie crust, baked
salt and pepper to taste
1/2 c. green onions, chopped
1/3 c. fresh basil, chopped
1/2 c. bacon, crisply cooked
   and crumbled
1 c. mayonnaise
1 c. shredded Cheddar cheese

Layer tomato slices in pie crust.
Season to taste with salt and pepper.
Top with onions, basil and bacon.
In a bowl, mix together mayonnaise
and cheese; spread over bacon. Bake,
uncovered, at 350 degrees for
30 minutes, or until lightly golden.
Serves 6 to 8.

283

Peggy Buckshaw
Stow, OH

This scrumptious pie
will be a hit at your
next get-together!

Ham & Cheese Strata

12 slices bread, crusts removed
1 lb. cooked ham, diced
2 c. shredded Cheddar cheese
6 eggs, beaten
3 c. milk
2 t. Worcestershire sauce
1 t. dry mustard
1/2 t. salt
1/4 t. pepper
1/8 t. cayenne pepper
1/4 c. onion, minced
1/4 c. green pepper, minced
1/4 c. butter, melted
1 c. corn flake cereal, crushed

Arrange 6 slices of bread in a single
layer in a greased 13"x9" baking pan;
top with ham and cheese. Cover with
remaining bread. In a bowl, beat
eggs, milk, Worcestershire sauce and
seasonings. Stir in onion and green
pepper; pour over bread mixture.
Cover and refrigerate overnight.
Remove from the refrigerator
30 minutes before baking. Drizzle
butter over casserole; sprinkle
with cereal. Bake, uncovered, at
350 degrees for about one hour,
or until a knife inserted near the
center comes out clean. Let stand
10 minutes before serving.
Serves 8 to 10.

Mary Gage
Wakewood, CA
The crushed corn flake
cereal adds a wonderful
crunch to this classic
make-ahead casserole!

Supreme Pizza Casserole

16-oz. pkg. rotini pasta,
  uncooked
2 15-oz. jars pizza sauce
2-1/4 oz. can sliced black olives,
  drained
4-oz. can sliced mushrooms,
  drained
1 green pepper, chopped
1 onion, chopped
20 to 30 pepperoni slices
2 c. shredded pizza-blend or
  Italian-blend cheese

Cook pasta according to package
directions; drain. Combine pasta
with remaining ingredients except
cheese. Transfer to a 13"x9" baking
pan; top with cheese. Bake,
uncovered, at 425 degrees for
20 to 25 minutes, until cheese is
golden and bubbly. Serves 8 to 10.

285

Tasha Petenzi
Goodlettsville, TN
This is a great recipe
for a potluck dinner or
an easy weeknight supper.

Mexican Braid

1 lb. ground turkey
10-oz. can diced tomatoes with
    green chiles, drained
1 onion, chopped
1 c. corn
2 loaves frozen bread dough,
    thawed
8-oz. pkg. shredded Pepper Jack
    cheese

Brown turkey with tomatoes and
onion in a skillet over medium heat;
drain. Add corn; cook until heated
through. Roll out each loaf of dough
to 1/4-inch thickness. Transfer to
baking sheets that have been lined
with lightly greased aluminum foil.
Cut diagonal slits along each side of
the dough, about one inch apart and
3 inches deep. Place half of turkey
mixture in the center of each piece
of dough. Top each with half of
cheese. Fold in short sides of dough,
pinching to seal. Fold dough flaps
over the turkey mixture, alternating
sides and creating a braided pattern.
Pinch edges to seal. Bake at
350 degrees for 25 to 30 minutes,
until golden. Serves 16.

Kristin Stone
Davis, CA

This is a recipe I created
for my husband. He loves
spicy foods, and this
braid hit the spot!

Cabbage Roll Casserole

2 lbs. ground beef, browned
1 c. onion, chopped
29-oz. can tomato sauce
1 head cabbage, chopped
1 c. instant rice, uncooked
1 t. salt
14-oz. can beef broth

Combine all ingredients except broth in an ungreased, deep 13"x9" baking pan. Drizzle with broth; cover with aluminum foil. Bake at 350 degrees for one hour; uncover and stir. Cover again; bake 30 additional minutes, or until rice is cooked and casserole is heated through. Makes 10 to 12 servings.

287

Dianne Gregory
Sheridan, AR

The flavors of a tasty favorite without all the fuss!

Pierogie Casserole

4 onions, chopped
6 T. butter, divided
10 potatoes, peeled and boiled
1/2 c. chicken broth
1/2 to 1 c. milk
salt and pepper to taste
2 eggs, beaten
1/4 c. shredded Colby cheese
1/2 c. shredded Cheddar cheese,
    divided
16-oz. pkg. mafalda or bowtie
    pasta, cooked

In a skillet over medium heat, sauté
onions in 2 tablespoons butter; set
aside. Mash potatoes with remaining
butter, broth, milk, salt and pepper.
Add eggs and cheeses, reserving some
cheese for topping; mix well. Layer
pasta, potato mixture and onion in a
greased 13"x9" baking pan. Top with
remaining cheese. Bake, uncovered,
at 350 degrees for 30 minutes, or
until heated through. Serves 12.

Cheryl Lagler
Zionsville, PA
Mafalda pasta is perfect in
this recipe if you have it
handy in the pantry.

Chicken Chestnut Casserole

6 boneless, skinless chicken
   breasts
1 t. salt
8-oz. can sliced water chestnuts,
   drained
2 10-3/4 oz. cans cream of
   mushroom soup
12-oz. pkg. shredded Cheddar
   cheese
2-oz. jar diced pimentos,
   drained
1 c. milk
7-oz. pkg. elbow macaroni,
   uncooked
1 onion, finely chopped

289

Cover chicken with water in a
medium saucepan; bring to a boil
over medium-high heat. Add salt
and simmer until chicken is tender.
Drain, reserving 1-1/2 cups broth
from the saucepan. Cube chicken;
set aside. Mix remaining ingredients
and reserved broth in a large bowl.
Fold in chicken and spread mixture
in a lightly greased 13"x9" baking
pan. Cover and refrigerate for at
least 12 hours. Bake, uncovered, at
325 degrees for one hour and
15 minutes. Serves 8 to 10.

Nancy Molldrem
Eau Claire, WI

A great make-ahead
dish...pure comfort food
at its finest.

Turkey & Wild Rice Quiche

1 c. wild rice, uncooked
1/3 c. green onions, chopped
1/4 c. red pepper, chopped
5 T. butter
10-inch deep-dish pie crust
1/2 lb. deli smoked turkey, diced
2 c. shredded Swiss cheese
6 eggs, beaten
1 c. half-and-half
1 T. Worcestershire sauce

Cook rice according to package directions; set aside. Sauté onions and red pepper in butter over medium heat until crisp-tender. In pie crust, layer turkey, onion mixture, cheese and rice. In a bowl, whisk together remaining ingredients; pour over rice. Bake, uncovered, at 400 degrees for 20 minutes. Reduce heat to 325 degrees and bake an additional 30 to 35 minutes. Remove from oven; let stand 15 minutes before cutting into wedges. Serves 6 to 8.

Angela Biggin
Lyons, IL

The combination of turkey and wild rice is a pleasant change from a traditional quiche.

Chile Relleno Casserole

7-oz. can whole green chiles,
   drained
16-oz. pkg. shredded Monterey
   Jack cheese, divided
16-oz. pkg. shredded Cheddar
   cheese, divided
7-oz. can chopped green chiles
salt and pepper to taste
6 eggs, beaten
13-oz. can evaporated milk
Optional: salsa and sour cream

291

Slit whole chiles and remove seeds;
rinse and dry. Lay whole chiles,
skin-side down, in a lightly greased
13"x9" baking pan; sprinkle with
half of each cheese. Top with
chopped chiles, remaining cheese,
salt and pepper. In a bowl, combine
eggs and milk; pour over top. Bake,
uncovered, at 350 degrees for
45 minutes. Serve with salsa or
sour cream, if desired. Serves 8.

Georgia Mallory
Fullerton, CA

This is a tasty breakfast,
brunch or anytime
casserole...yummy served
with sour cream, salsa and
lots of fresh melon!

Quick Beefy Bean & Biscuit Bake

1 lb. ground beef
1/2 c. onion, chopped
1 t. salt
1/2 t. pepper
28-oz. can brown sugar baked
  beans
1/4 c. barbecue sauce
1/4 c. catsup
1 c. shredded Cheddar cheese
16.3-oz. tube refrigerated
  buttermilk biscuits

In a skillet over medium heat, brown beef with onion, salt and pepper; drain. Stir in baked beans, barbecue sauce and catsup; spoon beef mixture into an ungreased 13"x9" baking pan. Sprinkle cheese evenly over top. Separate each biscuit into 2 thinner biscuits and arrange evenly on top. Bake, uncovered, at 350 degrees for 30 to 35 minutes, until bubbly and biscuits are golden. Makes 6 to 8 servings.

Hana Brosmer
Huntingburg, IN
Golden biscuits layered over a hearty filling make this meal satisfying.

Cheesy Chile Rice

2 c. water
2 c. instant rice, uncooked
16-oz. container sour cream
4-oz. can diced green chiles
3 c. shredded Cheddar cheese,
  divided

In a saucepan over medium-high heat, bring water to a boil. Stir in rice; remove from heat. Cover and let stand 5 minutes, until water is absorbed. In a large bowl, mix together rice, sour cream, chiles and 2 cups cheese. Spread in a greased 2-quart casserole dish; top with remaining cheese. Bake, uncovered, at 400 degrees for 30 minutes, or until cheese is melted and top is lightly golden. Makes 6 servings.

293

Wendy Reaume
Chatham, Ontario

When I was growing up, my mom made this simple rice dish whenever we had Mexican food for dinner. It's yummy with burritos and tortilla chips.

Rumbledethumps

1 lb. potatoes, peeled and diced
2 T. butter
1 onion, thinly sliced
2 c. cabbage, finely shredded
salt and pepper to taste
2/3 c. shredded Cheddar cheese,
   divided

Cover potatoes with water in a
saucepan; bring to a boil. Reduce
heat; cover and simmer for
8 minutes, or until just tender.
Drain and rinse under cold water;
drain again. Transfer potatoes to a
bowl; mash coarsely with a fork and
set aside. Heat butter in a skillet;
add onion and cook over low heat
for 10 minutes, or until soft. Add
cabbage; cook for 5 minutes. Stir in
potatoes, salt and pepper. Remove
from heat; stir in 2 tablespoons
cheese. Transfer to a greased
9"x9" baking pan; sprinkle with
remaining cheese. Bake, uncovered,
at 350 degrees for 20 minutes, or
until heated through. Serves 4 to 6.

Jane Finn
Gurnee, IL

A funny Scottish name for
a hearty, satisfying side!
Garnish with some crispy
bacon to make it even better!

Warm & Wonderful Chicken Salad

Susan Fracker
New Concord, OH

Perfect paired with fresh fruit and a warm muffin.

2 c. cooked chicken, shredded
2 c. celery, diced
1 T. onion, grated
1 c. mayonnaise
1/2 c. slivered almonds
1/2 t. lemon juice
1-1/2 c. shredded Cheddar
   cheese, divided
1/2 c. potato chips, crushed

Mix chicken, celery, onion, mayonnaise, almonds, lemon juice and one cup cheese in a greased 13"x9" baking pan. Top with remaining cheese and chips. Bake, uncovered, at 450 degrees for 15 to 20 minutes, until hot and bubbly. Serves 6 to 8.

Mushroom & Barley Casserole

3/4 c. quick-cooking barley,
  uncooked
1/2 c. onion, chopped
1/4 c. butter
4-oz. can sliced mushrooms
14-1/2 oz. can chicken broth
1/2 c. sliced almonds

In a saucepan, sauté barley and onion in butter until golden; spoon into a greased 1-1/2 quart casserole dish. Add undrained mushrooms and broth; mix well. Bake, covered, at 350 degrees for one hour and 15 minutes. Remove cover and sprinkle with almonds. Bake, uncovered, for an additional 15 minutes. Serves 4 to 6.

Anne Marie Verdiramo
Rochester, MN

My family loves this recipe!
It was even published
in my grandmother's
church cookbook.

Green Bean Delight

4 16-oz. cans green beans, drained
1-oz. pkg. ranch salad dressing mix
2 10-3/4 oz. cans cream of mushroom soup
1/4 c. milk
8-oz. pkg. shredded Colby Jack cheese
1 c. sliced almonds or cashews
2.8-oz. can French fried onions

Place green beans in a lightly greased 13"x9" baking pan; set aside. Combine dressing mix, soup and milk in a bowl; pour over beans. Sprinkle with cheese and nuts; top with onions. Bake, uncovered, at 350 degrees for 25 minutes. Serves 8 to 10.

297

Jackie Balla
Walbridge, OH

An old standby dressed up with shredded cheese and nuts.

Famous White Mac & Cheese

16-oz. pkg. elbow macaroni,
   uncooked
2 T. butter
2 T. all-purpose flour
3 c. milk
1 lb. Monterey Jack cheese, cubed
1/2 lb. Pepper Jack cheese, cubed

Cook macaroni according to package directions; drain and set aside. Meanwhile, melt butter in a saucepan over medium heat. Stir in flour until combined; add milk and stir until mixture boils. Remove from heat; add cheese and stir until melted. Combine cheese mixture and cooked macaroni; place in an ungreased 13"x9" baking pan. Bake, uncovered, at 350 degrees for 30 minutes, or until bubbly. Makes 8 servings.

Shannon James
Georgetown, KY

When my four kids come running in from playing and see that my mac & cheese is in the oven, it puts a smile on everyone's face.

Game-Day BBQ Onions

11-oz. pkg. mesquite barbecue-
  flavored potato chips, divided
2 10-3/4 oz. cans cream of
  chicken soup
1/2 c. milk
4 sweet onions, thinly sliced
  and divided
2 c. shredded sharp Cheddar
  cheese, divided

Crush 2 cups of potato chips; set
aside. Whisk together soup and
milk; set aside. Place half of
onion slices in the bottom of a
13"x9" baking pan coated with
non-stick vegetable spray. Spread
uncrushed chips over onions; add
one cup cheese and half of soup
mixture. Repeat layering. Top with
reserved crushed chips. Bake,
uncovered, at 350 degrees for
one hour. Serves 10.

299

Cheryl Breeden
North Platte, NE

So simple...a true football
night party favorite that
will turn anyone into
an onion lover.

Hashbrown Casserole

10-3/4 oz. can cream of
    chicken soup
8-oz. container sour cream
1/2 c. margarine, melted and
    divided
2 c. shredded sharp Cheddar
    cheese
salt and pepper to taste
30-oz. pkg. frozen shredded
    hashbrowns, thawed
1 c. corn flake cereal, crushed

In a bowl, combine soup, sour
cream, half the margarine, shredded
cheese, salt and pepper. Pour mixture
into a lightly greased 13"x9" baking
pan; top with hashbrowns. Mix
corn flake cereal and remaining
margarine; spread over hashbrowns.
Bake, uncovered, at 350 degrees for
30 minutes, or until hot and bubbly.
Serves 6.

Shelia Butts
Creedmoor, NC
Such a creamy, filling
side dish and it's
so easy to make.

Kale & Potato Casserole

1/4 c. butter, melted
3 potatoes, thinly sliced
10 leaves kale, finely chopped
5 T. grated Parmesan cheese
salt and pepper to taste

In a bowl, drizzle butter over potatoes and mix well. Grease a cast-iron skillet and arrange a layer of potatoes in the bottom. Top with 1/3 of the kale, 1/3 of the cheese, salt and pepper. Continue layering, ending with potatoes; sprinkle with remaining cheese. Cover with aluminum foil and bake at 375 degrees for 30 minutes. Remove foil and bake for another 15 to 30 minutes, until potatoes are tender. Serves 4 to 6.

Jill Ross
Gooseberry Patch

Warm potatoes, wilted greens and Parmesan cheese make this a hearty side!

Noodle Kugel

16-oz. pkg. wide egg noodles,
   uncooked
3/4 to 1 c. butter, melted
16-oz. container sour cream
20-oz. can crushed pineapple,
   drained
4 eggs, beaten
1 c. sugar
1/2 t. salt
2 t. vanilla extract
Optional: cinnamon

Cook noodles according to package
directions; drain. Combine noodles
and remaining ingredients in a
greased 13"x9" baking pan. Bake,
uncovered, at 350 degrees for one
hour, or until heated through. Top
with cinnamon, if using. Serves
10 to 12.

**Gail Flusche-Hill
Hammond, IN**
My whole family loves this
sweet dish... it's always
a hit every holiday!

White Cheddar-Cauliflower Casserole

1 head cauliflower, cooked and
   mashed
8-oz. pkg. shredded white
   Cheddar cheese, divided
1/2 lb. bacon, crisply cooked,
   crumbled and divided
1/2 c. cream cheese, softened
2 T. sour cream
salt and pepper to taste

Combine cauliflower, half the
Cheddar cheese and 3/4 of the bacon
in a bowl. Add cream cheese and sour
cream; mix well. Spread mixture in a
greased 8"x8" baking pan; top with
remaining cheese and bacon.
Sprinkle with salt and pepper. Bake,
uncovered, at 350 degrees for 20 to
25 minutes, until bubbly and golden
around edges. Serves 6.

303

Lisa Ashton
Aston, PA

Lots of cheese and bacon
will have the kids eating
their cauliflower in this
terrific casserole.

Scalloped Potatoes

3 potatoes, peeled and sliced
6 slices bacon, halved
1 onion, chopped
3 T. fried chicken coating mix
1/2 t. salt
2 c. milk
1 c. shredded Cheddar cheese

In a saucepan over medium heat,
cover potatoes with water and
cook until almost tender; drain.
Meanwhile, cook bacon and onion
in a skillet over medium heat. Drain,
reserving 2 tablespoons drippings.
Add coating mix, salt and milk to
reserved drippings; cook until
thickened. Fold potatoes into bacon
mixture. Transfer to a greased
3-1/2 quart casserole dish and bake,
covered, at 350 degrees for
30 minutes. Remove cover, top
with cheese and bake for another
15 minutes, or until cheese is melted.
Serves 6.

Lynnette Zaunmiller
San Tan Valley, AZ

My mother used to make this
recipe quite often...there
were three of us girls
and we all loved it!

Golden Macaroni & Cheese

10-3/4 oz. can cream of
   mushroom soup
1/2 c. milk
1/2 t. mustard
1/8 t. pepper
3 c. elbow macaroni, cooked
2 c. shredded Cheddar cheese,
   divided
1 c. French fried onions

Blend soup, milk, mustard and
pepper in a lightly greased 1-1/2 quart
casserole dish. Stir in macaroni and
1-1/2 cups cheese. Bake, uncovered,
at 350 degrees for 20 minutes. Top
with remaining cheese and onions;
bake 10 additional minutes. Serves 4.

305

Gale Harris
Fort Worth, TX
A topping of crispy
French fried onions gives
this traditional standby
extra crunch!

Butternut Squash Casserole

1 to 2 butternut squash, peeled
   and cubed
2 eggs, beaten
1/4 c. milk
2 T. butter, softened
1/2 c. sugar
1 t. vanilla
1/2 t. cinnamon
1/2 t. nutmeg

In a saucepan over medium-high heat, cover squash with water and cook until tender, about 7 to 9 minutes; drain. In a small bowl, beat squash until smooth. Add remaining ingredients; beat well. Spoon into a 2-quart casserole dish coated with non-stick vegetable spray. Cover and bake at 350 degrees for 30 to 35 minutes, until heated through. Serves 4 to 6.

Mary Patenaude
Griswold, CT

This is a wonderfully yummy addition to any meal. We especially love it around the holidays.

Cheesy Vegetable Casserole

2 16-oz. pkgs. frozen stir-fry
   blend vegetables, thawed
   and drained
16-oz. pkg. pasteurized process
   cheese spread
1/4 c. milk
1/2 c. butter
1 sleeve round buttery crackers,
   crushed

Place vegetables in a lightly greased
13"x9" baking pan; set aside. Melt
cheese in a saucepan over low heat;
add milk. Stir until smooth; pour
over vegetables. Melt butter and stir
in cracker crumbs; sprinkle over
vegetables. Bake, uncovered, at
350 degrees for 20 to 25 minutes,
until heated through. Makes 6 to
8 servings.

307

Colleen McAleavey
Plum, PA

We like to vary this
casserole by choosing
different blends of
frozen vegetables.

Scalloped Corn

1 onion, chopped
1/2 c. plus 1 T. butter, melted
14-3/4 oz. can creamed corn
2 11-oz. cans corn, drained
8-1/2 oz. pkg. corn muffin mix
dried parsley
salt and pepper to taste

In a skillet over medium heat, sauté
onion in butter until translucent.
Combine onion and remaining
ingredients in a lightly greased
13"x9" baking pan. Bake, uncovered,
at 350 degrees for 45 minutes to
one hour, until golden. Serves 8.

Barbara Pache
Marshall, WI

Grandmother made this
casserole for every family
reunion. It was always
everyone's favorite.

Cheesy Lentils & Rice Casserole

3/4 c. dried lentils, uncooked
1/2 c. long-cooking rice,
    uncooked
3 c. chicken broth
2 T. dried, minced onion
1/2 t. dried basil
1/4 t. dried oregano
1/4 t. dried thyme
1/4 t. garlic powder
3/4 c. shredded Cheddar cheese

Blend all ingredients except cheese
in a 2-quart casserole dish. Bake,
covered, at 300 degrees for one hour
and 15 minutes. Uncover and top
with cheese; bake for 15 minutes, or
until cheese is melted. Serves 4 to 6.

309

Shirley Howie
Foxboro, MA

This is such a delicious
low-fat casserole.
My husband requests it
all the time!

Spinach Casserole

2 10-oz. pkgs. frozen chopped
spinach, thawed and drained
salt and pepper to taste
10-3/4 oz. can cream of
mushroom soup
8-oz. container sour cream
3/4 c. frozen chopped pepper,
onion & celery mix
1/2 sleeve round buttery
crackers, crushed
3 eggs, beaten
2 c. shredded Cheddar cheese,
divided

Place spinach in a large bowl; season
with salt and pepper. Combine
remaining ingredients, reserving
1/2 cup cheese. Pour mixture into a
lightly greased 2-quart casserole dish.
Bake, uncovered, at 350 degrees for
45 minutes, or until center is set.
Top with remaining cheese. Bake for
an additional 10 minutes, or until
cheese is melted. Serves 8 to 10.

Kay Daugherty
Collinsville, MS

This yummy casserole
is expected at every
family gathering!

Broccoli & Rice Casserole

1 c. long-cooking rice, uncooked
1 onion, chopped
3 stalks celery, chopped
1 c. butter, divided
10-oz. pkg. frozen chopped
    broccoli, thawed and drained
16-oz. jar pasteurized process
    cheese sauce
10-3/4 oz. can cream of
    mushroom soup
1 c. sour cream
1 sleeve round buttery crackers,
    crushed

Cook rice according to package
directions; set aside. Sauté onion
and celery for 3 minutes in 1/2 cup
butter. Mix all ingredients except
remaining butter and crackers in a
greased 2-quart casserole dish; top
with crackers. Melt remaining butter
and drizzle over crackers. Bake,
uncovered, at 350 degrees for
35 minutes, or until heated
through. Serves 8.

Patricia Elmore
Bessemer City, NC

I have been cooking this
dish for my family for
over 40 years, and they still
get excited to see this
loved dish on the table.

Minnesota Carrot-Asparagus Bake

1-1/2 c. carrots, peeled and
   chopped
1 c. onion, sliced
16-oz. jar pasteurized process
   cheese sauce
3 T. butter, melted
3 T. all-purpose flour
1-1/2 c. milk
1 t. salt
1 t. pepper
10-oz. pkg. frozen asparagus,
   thawed and drained
2.8-oz. can French fried onions

Combine carrots and onion in a
saucepan. Cover with water and boil
until almost tender; drain and set
aside. In a bowl, mix together cheese
sauce, butter, flour and milk; add salt
and pepper. Set aside. Layer carrot
mixture and asparagus in a greased
9"x9" baking pan; drizzle cheese
mixture over top. Sprinkle with
onions. Bake, uncovered, at
350 degrees for 15 to 20 minutes,
until heated through. Serves 8.

Mary Scurti
Highland, CA

We make this yummy
casserole year 'round, but
it is definitely a tradition
at our holiday table.

Sweet Potato-Apple Bake

4 sweet potatoes, boiled, peeled
   and sliced
1/2 c. butter
1/2 c. sugar
1/2 c. brown sugar, packed
1 to 2 t. cinnamon
4 tart apples, peeled, cored
   and sliced
1/2 c. water
1/4 c. lemon juice
1/4 c. orange juice

Arrange a layer of sliced potatoes
in a greased one-quart casserole dish;
dot with butter and sprinkle with
sugar, brown sugar and cinnamon.
Arrange a layer of apple slices on
top; continue layering until all
ingredients except water and juices
are used. Combine water and juices;
pour over top. Cover and bake at
400 degrees for 45 minutes, or
until apples are tender. Makes 4 to
6 servings.

313

Wendy Jacobs
Idaho Falls, ID

This is a really tasty
change from the traditional
sweet potato casseroles
we're used to.

Savory Rice Casserole

4-oz. can sliced mushrooms,
  drained and liquid reserved
8-oz. can sliced water chestnuts,
  drained and liquid reserved
1/2 c. butter
1 c. long-cooking rice, uncooked
10-1/2 oz. can French onion
  soup

In a skillet over medium heat, sauté mushrooms and water chestnuts in butter; set aside. Add uncooked rice to an ungreased one-quart casserole dish. Stir in soup, mushroom mixture and reserved liquids. Bake, covered, at 375 degrees for 45 to 60 minutes, until rice is tender. Serves 6 to 8.

Kathy Dassel
Newburgh, IN

My sister-in-law gave me this delicious recipe while we were visiting her in Raleigh, North Carolina.

Pineapple Casserole

20-oz. can crushed pineapple
20-oz. can pineapple chunks,
   drained
2 c. shredded sharp Cheddar
   cheese
1/4 c. sugar
6 T. all-purpose flour
1 sleeve round buttery crackers,
   crushed
1/2 c. butter, melted
Optional: pineapple rings,
   maraschino cherries

Mix together all ingredients except
crackers and butter in a greased
13"x9" baking pan. Top with
crackers; drizzle butter over top.
Bake, uncovered, at 350 degrees for
about 30 minutes, or until heated
through and bubbly. Garnish with
pineapple rings and cherries, if
desired. Serves 8.

Lynn Filipowicz
Wilmington, NC

I have been making this
dish for years...it's good
hot or cold.

315

Fabulous Baked Potato Casserole

6 to 7 potatoes, peeled and cubed
2 c. shredded Cheddar cheese
1 c. mayonnaise
1/2 c. sour cream
1 onion, diced
6 slices bacon, crisply cooked
    and crumbled

In a large saucepan, boil potatoes
in water until fork-tender, about
20 minutes; drain and set aside to
cool. Combine cheese, mayonnaise,
sour cream and onion; mix in
potatoes, tossing gently to coat.
Spread potato mixture in a buttered
13"x9" baking pan; sprinkle bacon on
top. Bake, uncovered, at 350 degrees
until golden and bubbly, about 20 to
25 minutes. Serves 8.

Ginia Johnston
Greeneville, TN

Make sure to get some quick,
because this delectable dish
always disappears first
at every gathering!

Zucchini-Corn Casserole

3 lbs. zucchini, cubed
2 c. corn
1 onion, chopped
1 green pepper, chopped
2 T. butter
salt and pepper to taste
4 eggs, lightly beaten
1 c. shredded Cheddar cheese
paprika to taste

In a saucepan, cook zucchini in boiling water for 2 to 3 minutes; drain and set aside. In a skillet over medium heat, sauté corn, onion and green pepper in butter until crisp-tender. Remove from heat and add zucchini to corn mixture; season with salt and pepper and let cool slightly. Stir in eggs and transfer to a greased 13"x9" baking pan. Top with cheese and paprika. Bake, uncovered, at 350 degrees for 40 minutes, or until lightly golden and bubbly. Serves 6 to 8.

317

Dani Simmers
Kendallville, IN
This recipe came from my friend's great-aunt...it tastes wonderful and is pretty easy to fix, too!

INDEX

INDEX

INDEX

INDEX

Sandwiches

Sides

INDEX

Soups

U.S. to Metric Recipe Equivalents

Volume Measurements

1/4 teaspoon	1 mL
1/2 teaspoon	2 mL
1 teaspoon	5 mL
1 tablespoon = 3 teaspoons	15 mL
2 tablespoons = 1 fluid ounce	30 mL
1/4 cup	60 mL
1/3 cup	75 mL
1/2 cup = 4 fluid ounces	125 mL
1 cup = 8 fluid ounces	250 mL
2 cups = 1 pint =16 fluid ounces	500 mL
4 cups = 1 quart	1 L

Weights

1 ounce	30 g
4 ounces	120 g
8 ounces	225 g
16 ounces = 1 pound	450 g

Oven Temperatures

300° F	150° C
325° F	160° C
350° F	180° C
375° F	190° C
400° F	200° C
450° F	230° C

Baking Pan Sizes

Square

8x8x2 inches	2 L = 20x20x5 cm
9x9x2 inches	2.5 L = 23x23x5 cm

Rectangular

13x9x2 inches	3.5 L = 33x23x5 cm

Loaf

9x5x3 inches	2 L = 23x13x7 cm

Round

8x1-1/2 inches	1.2 L = 20x4 cm
9x1-1/2 inches	1.5 L = 23x4 cm

Recipe Abbreviations

t. = teaspoon	ltr. = liter
T. = tablespoon	oz. = ounce
c. = cup	lb. = pound
pt. = pint	doz. = dozen
qt. = quart	pkg. = package
gal. = gallon	env. = envelope

Kitchen Measurements

A pinch = 1/8 tablespoon	1 fluid ounce = 2 tablespoons
3 teaspoons = 1 tablespoon	4 fluid ounces = 1/2 cup
2 tablespoons = 1/8 cup	8 fluid ounces = 1 cup
4 tablespoons = 1/4 cup	16 fluid ounces = 1 pint
8 tablespoons = 1/2 cup	32 fluid ounces = 1 quart
16 tablespoons = 1 cup	16 ounces net weight = 1 pound
2 cups = 1 pint	
4 cups = 1 quart	
4 quarts = 1 gallon	

Our Story

Back in 1984, we were next-door neighbors raising our families in the little town of Delaware, Ohio. Two moms with small children, we were looking for a way to do what we loved and stay home with the kids too. We had always shared a love of home cooking and making memories with family & friends and so, after many a conversation over the backyard fence, **Gooseberry Patch** was born.

We put together our first catalog at our kitchen tables, enlisting the help of our loved ones wherever we could. From that very first mailing, we found an immediate connection with many of our customers and it wasn't long before we began receiving letters, photos and recipes from these new friends. In 1992, we put together our very first cookbook, compiled from hundreds of these recipes and, the rest, as they say, is history.

Hard to believe it's been over 25 years since those kitchen-table days! From that original little **Gooseberry Patch** family, we've grown to include an amazing group of creative folks who love cooking, decorating and creating as much as we do. Today, we're best known for our homestyle, family-friendly cookbooks, now recognized as national bestsellers.

One thing's for sure, we couldn't have done it without our friends all across the country. Each year, we're honored to turn thousands of your recipes into our collectible cookbooks. Our hope is that each book captures the stories and heart of all of you who have shared with us. Whether you've been with us since the beginning or are just discovering us, welcome to the **Gooseberry Patch** family!

JoAnn & Vickie

Visit us online:
www.gooseberrypatch.com
1·800·854·6673